Couples:
The Art of Staying Together

Couples:
The Art of Staying Together

Anita and Robert Taylor, M.D.

Published by ACROPOLIS BOOKS LTD. • WASHINGTON, D.C. 20009

ACROPOLIS BOOKS LTD.
Colortone Building, 2400 17th St., N.W., Washington, D.C. 20009

Printed in the United States of America by
COLORTONE PRESS Creative Graphics, Inc.
Washington, D.C. 20009

Library of Congress Cataloging in Publication Data

Taylor, Anita, 1940-
   Couples.

   Bibliography: p.
   Includes index.
   1. Marriage. 2. Unmarried couples—Case studies. 3. Interpersonal relations—
Case studies. 4. Stress (Physiology) I. Taylor, Robert B., joint author. II. Title.
HQ734.T257 301.41 78-6976
ISBN 0-87491-219-9

This book is lovingly dedicated to our daughters
Diana and Sharon

TABLE OF CONTENTS

Table of Contents ● 7

E VERYONE IS CONCERNED today about marriage breaking down, and almost everyone has a remedy for the problem. The Taylors have performed a service to society by proposing a simple, straightforward and logical method of understanding what is actually happening—in marriage, and in other kinds of "couples" as well. The greatest strength of the book is in showing the reader that almost everyone is a part of a "couple," such as two roommates, or an aged parent and a care-taking offspring, or two people working closely together on a job. This comparison lifts the discussion of relationship conflicts out of the usual clichés and helps one to view one's own involvement with more clarity and less emotional bias.

Couples is a positive book, unlike many popular books on marriage that offer dazzling though confusing analyses of the complexities of unconscious motivation. It assumes that people do have resources within themselves and that they can make changes in their lives. Likewise it assumes that making the effort to understand what is going on (using the simple sets of self-ratings the Taylors have created) is in itself an important first step in changing.

As a professional marriage counselor who has seen numerous examples of the problems the Taylors write about, I believe that this book can help many people from different walks of life understand and improve whatever "couples" they are part of.

Dr. David Balderston, Ed.D.

New York City

Member, American Association of Marriage and Family Counselors

When a man meets his mate, society begins
Ralph Waldo Emerson

W*HAT HAPPENS TO COUPLES seems more apparent in a small town: The church pew where a family sat each Sunday stands empty following a divorce; a son leaves home to escape from his father after constant arguing creates a chasm that can not be bridged; partners in a construction company dissolve their association after 15 years, as divergent goals lead to irreconcilable differences. And all the while, tongues wag and oldtimers shake their heads in dismay.*

Of course, good news travels fast too. A couple who had been separated come together to a party; a neighbor's daughter brings her roommate home from college for the holidays; a surprise wedding anniversary party is planned.

For 14 years in a small-town medical office we have seen one-to-one relationships form, falter, then recover or wither. Individually or by two's people have sought advice when their couple unions were in trouble, and at these times we often wondered: Why did these two people form a couple? What needs were met? Can or even should they continue as a couple? Would there have been any way to predict the trouble being faced? Have these persons considered the implications of their alternatives, the outcomes of staying together or ending the relationship? And can what we learn from one couple be used to help others?

Our book aims to answer these questions. We offer insight gained from long-term observation of more than 900 couples. From this continuing involvement we have formulated a theory that can help predict couple continuity—or separation—and which may allow action before problems become overwhelming. We present a method of analyzing the outcome of the choices presented: What are the real implications to the person and to society when a couple split? We propose that by careful analysis and by action couples can improve their lives together and can avoid the emotional upheaval of an unplanned couple termination.

Marriage and the family are popular topics and many books have been written describing these institutions. However, our study of one-to-one relationships led us to the realization that there are a number of couple alternatives to the husband-wife stereotype, in itself not a startling revelation, and, more important, that analytical criteria can be applied to traditional and alternative couple relationships with equal validity. Thus, using the approach described in the following chapters, it is possible to examine not only Mr. and Mrs. Middle Class America, but also the couple relationships of a mother and daughter, plumber and apprentice, homosexuals on a one-night stand, and the dating couple contemplating marriage.

Books, like all forms of art, are an outgrowth of the times. A book such as this would not have been written a generation ago, because at that time couple relationships were tacitly presumed permanent. Romances continued happily ever after, marriage was forever, and business contracts had no termination clause. During the past two decades we have seen the advent of the era of disposability. Use it once and throw it away. In the medical office the doctor uses disposable needles, disposable syringes, and disposable patient gowns. Beverage bottles are emptied and discarded, and we have come to accept built-in obsolescence in the products that we purchase. Over these same two decades there developed a growing sense that human relationships were equally disposable, that personal bonds can be readily severed, as if removing an annoying thread from clothing. When convenience dictated, marriages were dissolved, contracts broken, and friendships terminated. It became more important to put a man on the moon than to spend time talking with a neighbor. Science became a powerful god and technology threatened to stifle humanism in our academic institutions and in our lives.

But over the past few years there has been a resurgence of interest in human values. Here and there medical philosophers are reaffirming that caring is as important as curing and that physicians must attend to the patient as well as to his disease. Businesses have recognized that human relationships—a feeling of a company "family"—can in fact boost dollar figures on the bottom line. In this direction, the young people have held a mirror to the middle generation and asked, "While you have been getting and spending, what has happened to your lives? Look what progress has done to your human values and relationships." And thus the world is reaffirming the value of continuing, caring relationships that occur between living, breathing persons.

The following chapters present a theory telling what keeps these continuing, caring relationships intact in times of stress. Because the subject of couple continuity is one of the most vital day by day problems in an individual's life, we have presented our theories as a serious work, free of clever slogans and literary embellishments. This book should be read—and reread—slowly, with time to assimilate the contents of each chapter before proceeding to the next. To aid the reader in identification of the most salient points, each chapter is preceded by topic questions that direct attention to the concepts presented. The book's appendix includes worksheets that allow the reader to apply the theories developed to his or her own couple relationships.

We believe that this is the first book that covers the full spectrum of couple relationships and that tells about the continuity of couples in our lives. Whether you live in a small town or large city, you will see yourself and your friends as couples in this book. We hope to help keep these couples together and strengthen their relationships.

Anita D. Taylor
Robert B. Taylor, M.D.

AS YOU BEGIN THIS BOOK, we want to focus your thinking on the couples in your life, and to do so, you should analyze one of your couple relationships in depth. Here is how: Select one of your own couple unions (any person with whom you have continuing interaction). It could be a parent, spouse, child, companion, friend, co-worker, and so forth. Record your answers to each of the following questions:

I. Why do you have this relationship? What need(s) does it meet?
    A. Biologic—there is physical intimacy that is not necessarily sexual
    B. Psychologic—there is emotional support and companionship
    C. Sociologic—there is an activity requiring a partner
    D. Economic—there is monetary investment, division of labor, or sharing of responsibility

II. What is the level of closeness between the two of you?
+1 A. The relationship fills a temporary and mundane need (Convenience)
+2 B. There is some personal involvement in the relationship (Supportive)

+3   C.   There is an increased sense of commitment and closeness with an expectation that the relationship will continue (Nurturative)

+4   D.   The couple is viewed as "permanent" and worth individual sacrifices (Unitive)

III.   Where do you place your relationship in the following stages?

+3   A.   The "honeymoon" or beginning stage (Commitment)

+2   B.   The period of adjustment (Accommodation)

+1   C.   The time of questioning as to whether to continue the couple relationship (Assessment)

+4   D.   The time when a decision has been made to continue the relationship after evaluating the alternatives (Recommitment)

IV.   What stress affects your couple relationship now?

-1   A.   Concerning an object—food, clothing, shelter, or money

-2   B.   Concerning an activity—planning, doing, moving, or staying

-3   C.   Concerning values, roles, or some relationship outside the couple—role changes, family decisions, health, or legal problems

-4   D.   Concerning couple unity—separation, infidelity, institutionalization, sexual dysfunction, or incompatible life goals

V.   How are each of you handling the stress?

-2   A.   Harmful handling of both partners—fighting, blaming, punishing, and so forth

1   B.   Harmful handling by one partner

0   C.   Denying existence of a problem

+1   D.   Recognizing the problem by one partner

+2   E.   Recognizing and openly discussing the problem by both partners

+3   F.   Trying to solve the problem with communication techniques or counseling

VI.   What kind of "family" or other outside support do each of you have for the couple relationship?

+2   A.   Both families approve

+1   B.   One family approves

0   C.   There is indifference

-1   D.   One family disapproves

-2   E.   Both familes disapprove

The numbers in the left margin represent values assigned to the various aspects of your couple relationship. Add the values. A plus score indicates a healthy relationship; a minus score suggests that couple bonds are in jeopardy. Save your answers and net score for comparison with your responses after finishing the book.

**COUPLE
FOCUS
CHAPTER
ONE**

1. What is a couple?

2. What are the five main aspects of
    couple dynamics?

3. What are the major couple rela-
    tionships in your life?

1

WHY DOES ANY COUPLE separate? Does the rift arise in the nature of the relationship or in the problems two people must face together? Why do some unions survive major crises while others crumble when faced with minor stress? And what can be done to keep couples together?

Keeping couples together is vital to the individuals involved and to society as well, because just as the selection of a mate begins society, the unplanned disruption of any union weakens the foundations of our social structure. During the past decade, separation of couples has reached epidemic proportions. For example, the United States divorce rate for married women over 15 years of age increased from 9 per 1,000 in 1955 to 20.3 per 1,000 in 1975; the National Center for Health Statistics tells us that more than two percent of the adult married women in America will be divorced during the current year.[23]* These divorces will affect the lives of more than three million persons, including more than 1.1 million children under the age of 18 years.[23]

Vital statistics describe only those couple events that are reported to the statisticians, namely marriages and divorces. It is

---

*Numbers in parentheses refer to works listed on pages 207-208.

socially and psychologically upsetting when other kinds of couples terminate, whether they are two persons living together, working together as a team, or involved in a partnership venture.

For each of these couples there may come a time when one or both mates say: "This is the end! We can't go on this way any longer." A married entertainment team decide that the advantages of divorce outweigh the joint financial loss involved. Two working girls sharing an apartment decide to go their separate ways before the lease ends. Partners in a corner grocery store go out of business.

What prompts these persons to end their couple relationships? Can the causes be identified, and the divorce (or other form of couple termination) be predicted? With early recognition of couple problems, can prompt action save the union? Can couple problems—and hence couple dissolution—be prevented?

This book proposes that the likelihood of couple termination or continuation is predictable in a given stress situation. It identifies several key aspects of the couple relationship which have a strong influence on whether a couple can weather a particular crises. It also shows that how partners respond to stress has an important impact on their staying power. Analysis of the couple relationship allows early problem recognition, guides remedial efforts, and—most important—may suggest ways to enhance and strengthen the couple union.

WHAT IS A COUPLE?

A couple is any union of two persons which forms to fill mutual needs and which persists for a measurable period of time. The needs filled may be trivial or profound and the duration of the relationship may be fleeting or enduring. Two single diners who share a table for two in a crowded restaurant are a couple; so are the man and woman celebrating their 50th wedding anniversary. While for these two couples there are vast differences in degrees of personal involvement and in duration, the two diverse unions share some common characteristics of all couples.

The traditional and most familiar couple has been the male-female, husband-wife relationship. Whether or not the union has been sanctified or legitimatized by church or state is of little importance. In Rome at the time of the Caesars, in an Australian aboriginal tribe, or in twentieth century America, the most common long-term couple has been the union of woman and man.

Emerson wrote more than a hundred years ago, "When man meets his mate, society begins." Mate can also mean comrade, associate, or partner, as well as spouse, and during the century since Emerson penned these words, a growing constellation of couple relationships has evolved. These relationships go beyond the shared search for food, shelter, and protection and meet the rising needs for self-expression, personal growth, and individual identity. Thus the mixed doubles tennis team, two divorced men living together, two strangers sharing a hospital room, and co-chairpersons of a political committee are couples just as surely as the middle-aged husband and wife are.

COUPLE DYNAMICS

In this study, couples are identified according to three key variables—whether the individuals are of the same or opposite sex, the same or different generation, and involved in a sexual or asexual relationship. The various combinations of these three variables led us to recognize eight couple categories. Other criteria were considered—such as whether or not there were blood ties, and whether or not the individuals were married—but these did not prove to be meaningful or helpful in our study.

Couple unions may be of long or brief duration, superficial or deep in intensity, mandated or freely negotiated, supportive or destructive, pleasurable or agonizing, familiar or bizarre. Whatever the nature of the relationship, the commitment of two people to form a couple initiates couple dynamics that are independent of the individuals. The couple, based upon the goals, efforts, and interactions of the two people involved, has a life of its own and encounters changes both predictable and unexpected. Five aspects of couple dynamics can be identified and measured: interaction level, stage in the couple life cycle, kind of stress faced, adaptive mechanisms, and family support systems.

Couple partners relate to one another at one of four *interactional levels*. Couples may progress from more superficial to deeper interactional levels, or—usually following a major problem in the relationship—may regress to more superficial interactional levels. The former change usually occurs with the progress from dating through engagement to marriage; the latter is seen as the interaction shift occurring between marriage and divorce. The interaction level may be determined by the nature of the relationship, as with business colleagues, or may be a common goal of the two individuals, as in a joint effort between psychiatrist and patient to delve deeply into emotions.

Each couple passes through progressive stages of a *couple life cycle,* and understanding these stages can help in estimating the strength of the couple union. The early stage of commitment gives way to discovery of flaws that require accommodation. This is followed by a period of reassessment, at which time the union is in greatest jeopardy. If the couple survives the critical evaluation, its chances for continuation are excellent indeed.

All couple relationships meet *stress* of various types. The business partners, the entertainment duo, or the roommates would remain together except for the impact of stress upon the relationship. Couples in a doctor's office describe many types of stress, including divergent goals, financial loss, separation, and infidelity. All of these stresses have varying (and measurable) influences upon couple stability.

Stress is met with some type of *adaptive method,* which may work to the couple's benefit or may just make matters worse. The married couple or business partners who make a poor investment may argue and blame each other, or may join forces to overcome the loss. Arguing will not correct the loss and can only harm the relationship, while cooperation may overcome the financial difficulty and build a stronger couple union.

Standing behind each couple is a *family support* system, which may show approval or disapproval. Although not of quite the same importance as the stages of the couple life cycle and type of stress, family support is nevertheless a significant influence upon the couple union. Family favor or disfavor becomes evident early in the relationship, and may be decisive in time of stress.

EIGHT REPRESENTATIVE COUPLES

This book discusses what happens to couples. It describes the nature of the couple relationship and presents the five aspects of couple dynamics. It also identifies eight significant couple categories and depicts one representative couple from each major category during a time of stress. It shows how they met that stress at their particular level of interaction and couple life cycle stage, and how family support or disapproval influenced the outcome.

Couple stability occurs when the factors favoring couple continuity outweigh those that threaten couple continuity. The following chapters describe these factors and their influence upon the couple in time of stress, as exemplified by the stories of the following eight couples:

1. Harry and Jane: Both in their mid 30's, married, and the parents of two children, Harry and Jane were what most would consider an average middle class couple. They enjoyed family outings, attended church regularly, and were both active in their community.

2. Roger and Gloria: For 15 years Gloria and Roger worked together side by side as waitress and restaurant owner. Neither was married, and their relationship was cordial yet professional. Both in their late 50's and facing the prospect of eventual retirement, a proposed change in working hours strained the relationship.

3. John and Margaret: Despite thinning hair and thanks to daily exercise, John looked younger than his 53 years; but still not as youthful as his pert 25-year-old second wife, Margaret. They laughed and touched like the newlyweds

they were, as family and friends shook their heads in disapproval.

4. Joseph and Maria: At age 36, Maria was the unmarried daughter of immigrant parents, living with her widower father. A marriage prospect arose, and affected the relationship between father and daughter.

5. George and Frank: Both in their late 40's, George and Frank had a long-standing homosexual relationship. They had achieved an enviable state of economic and emotional interdependence that was threatened by a financial obligation.

6. Charles and Michael: Although both in their late teens, these college roommates were as different as could be. Tall, blond, and noisy Charles and shorter, dark-haired, studious Michael made an odd couple indeed.

7. Phyllis and Nancy: Phyllis as professor and Nancy as her student were engaged in a close but covert homosexual relationship that was threatened by Nancy's impending graduation.

8. Lucille and Martha: At age 62, Lucille opened her home to her divorced daughter and three grandchildren. A couple union formed, based on family ties and mutual needs, but threatened by generational differences in childrearing.

These eight pairs selected as examples of the eight couple categories are composites of couples studied clinically. The most common type was the couple exemplified by Harry and Jane—the married, parenting husband and wife. The seven other couple types occurred less frequently in our practice, yet were also meaningful to the individuals involved as well as to our study.

Of the eight couples presented here, six lived together at the time described and two lived apart. Two couples were engaged in heterosexual relationships, two in homosexual relationships, and four couples had no sexual involvement. Four of the couples were from the same and four from differing generations. Two couples were bound by blood ties and six were not.

THE COUPLE STABILITY INDEX

As various facets of these couple relationships are presented, numerical values can be applied to determine couple stability. Numerical values are assigned to various stages of the five critical factors in the couple relationship: interaction, stage of couple life cycle, stress, adaption to stress, and support systems. The sum of these values gives the Couple Stability Index. A total of greater than zero indicates probability the couple will stay together, and a total of less than zero suggests that the couple will probably split in response to a particular stress.

A summary of the Couple Stability Index Values for each couple is found in the Appendix (see pages 182-197) and can be referred to as these couples and their conflicts are described through the next nine chapters.

COUPLE FOCUS: CHAPTER TWO

1. What spoken and unspoken agreements bond two people?

2. What paths do couples follow?

3. What needs are met by being a couple?

4. What factors keep a troubled union intact?

CHAPTER TWO: THE COUPLE ALLIANCE

2

W E BEGIN FORMING COUPLE alliances at birth. The earliest couple relationship is between the newborn infant and mother; there soon follows an interaction with father and perhaps with brother or sister. During childhood the youngster forms couple relationships with peers and adults important in his life, including teachers and extended family members. In adolescence, changes in the parent-child relationship coincide with the formation of intense couple bonds with peers of the same and opposite sex: best friends and first romances. During young adulthood one of these couple associations may mature into a continuing commitment involving common long-term goals, cohabitation, or marriage, and perhaps raising a family. Parenting affects the marital couple relationship, as does the eventual emancipation and departure of the offspring. As the children of parenting couples leave for work, college, or marriage, the partners enter a period in which they discover and re-examine one another, and perhaps establish a new relationship.[13] During middle age and late life the couple relationship may end by departure or death of one of the partners, which is often followed by the establishment of new couple relationships. Even late life is characterized by striving for one-to-one interaction, and persons in nursing homes often form couples with one another or with members of the staff.

THE COUPLE CONTRACT

Each couple lives by a contract, an agreement which is both expressed and implied, and which is governed by needs, goals, and social customs. The expressed contract may be as formal as a partnership agreement or marriage license. Or it may be as informal as the offer and acceptance of a movie date. There is an expressed contract between employer and employee, teacher and pupil, man and woman embarking upon a weekend together, or individuals of the same sex sharing an apartment. Within the bounds of social custom, the expressed couple contract is subject to considerable individual variation as evidenced by the wide variety of prenuptial agreements, business pacts, and living arrangements seen today. The agreement may be broken by either partner at any time.

The implied couple contract is strongly influenced by cultural mores, and is usually an unspoken understanding that actions will follow certain rules. Thus with the formal marital contract comes the implied agreement that these two individuals will live together, share their assets, and work for common goals. Within a business partnership there is the implied contract that neither partner will steal goods nor embezzle profits. Two individuals of the same sex who agree to share an apartment may do so with the implied understanding that they will lead more-or-less separate lives, and that neither has a long-term obligation to the other.

In time a couple contract may be renegotiated. This usually happens following a period of conflict, the outcome of which necessitates a change in the relationship. Within the traditional marital relationship, renegotiation of the couple contract may bring husband and wife to a deeper level of interaction—with a formal agreement to end a period of separation, achieve sobriety, or combat a financial disaster, combined with an implied agreement to show more caring and consideration for one another. On the other hand, renegotiation as a couple may bring the two partners a more superficial level of involvement with a formal contract to provide child support payments and establish visiting privileges, and with an implied agreement to avoid interfering with one another's lives (and new couple relationships). Business-related couples may undertake contract renegotiations when one partner gets a formal promotion, with the implied agreement that the promotion brings that partner greater status in the one-to-one relationship.

THE COUPLE TRAJECTORY

The behavioral sciences borrow many concepts from the physical disciplines; one is the idea of trajectory, meaning the course followed by a body moving under the action of given forces. For each couple union there is a trajectory, a path and devotion determined initially by the couple contract and subject to changes in the five aspects of couple dynamics. The trajectory can be described in terms of the degree and duration of interpersonal involvement.

The couple trajectory of a teenage girl and boy who contract for an evening movie date involves several hours together, a superficial interaction, and no continuing commitment. Their couple trajectory rises to a low level for several hours then returns to near the base line (see Figure 1, page 198).

A variable level of involvement is seen in two individuals of the same sex who will be dormitory roommates for the scholastic year. The couple trajectory of these two individuals may surpass the height of the dating couple, and persist for the school year duration by formal contractual agreement (see Figure 1, page 198).

A somewhat higher level of involvement is plotted for two business partners who work together daily, and the curve of their trajectory will extend indefinitely unless the formal contract calls for dissolution at a specific time (see Figure 1, page 198). A similar indefinite duration at an even greater level of involvement is projected for the married couple and for many individuals living together (see Figure 1, page 198).

When a couple trajectory is completed, the relationship ends without societal loss or psychological impact. Thus when the dating couple say goodnight and the roommates separate at the school year's end, their couple contracts and trajectories have been completed. Problems occur when the couple contract is broken and the trajectory is not completed, as with death, divorce, dissolution of a formal contract, violation of an implied contract, or other major disruption of the couple relationship.

Conversely, the couple's trajectory can be augmented— both in height and duration of the curve—by renegotiation of the couple contract or by changes in one or more aspects of couple dynamics.

COUPLE CONTINUITY

The couple relationship has many similarities to a legal corporation. When two or more individuals join to form a business corporation, a new entity is created. The corporation has a history, existence, and future of its own, independent of the shareholders and directors. Once formed, a couple is an entity apart from the new partners. The relationship begins a life cycle, is subject to stress, may indeed become "ill," and may recover or die. Recovery and survival of an ailing couple union is favored by four factors: (1) individual needs met by the relationship, (2) fears, (3) support systems, and (4) inertia.

Needs Met By a Couple

Two persons become a couple to meet specific needs, and if these needs continue to be met, it is likely that the relationship will complete its trajectory. For example, restauranteur Roger and waitress Gloria met one another's continuing needs to earn a livelihood while middle-aged John and his younger bride Margaret filled each other's physical and financial requirements. All other things being equal, if Roger had acquired sudden wealth through inheritance and sold his business to another, his couple relationship with Gloria would have terminated. Requiring continuing employment, Gloria would probably have joined another restaurant owner; or the realization that they were leaving each other might have led Roger and Gloria into a more personal—even romantic—union, with a new couple contract.

In the relationship between John and Margaret, based on an exchange of youthful attractiveness for middle-aged affluence, the loss of either asset would have severely strained and possibly broken the couple bonds as the needs of one or both failed to be met on a continuing basis.

What needs are filled by the couple union? They can be categorized as biologic, psychologic, sociologic, and economic.

BIOLOGIC NEEDS. Biologic needs met by the couple relationship may be as fundamental as reproduction and child-rearing. Equally compelling biologic needs include food, clothing, shelter, and protection. Couple relationships fulfilling biologic needs will involve some physical intimacy, though not necessarily sexual in nature. Biologic needs are part of the relationships between mother and child, the child caring for an aging parent, the nurse or doctor and patient, and perhaps between a housekeeper and employer.

PSYCHOLOGIC NEEDS. Partners can and should fill one another's psychologic needs for approval and validation of self-worth. They can provide emotional support in times of adversity and the security of knowing that another person cares. The psychologic need for companionship is great at all ages and often provides a major impetus to couple formation, particularly during the later years. Couple agreement concerning psychologic needs is usually implied, and meeting psychologic needs is as vital to the relationship as fulfilling biologic needs. Thus a short couple life expectancy could be predicted for the couple who make physical love by night, but attack one another's self-worth by day.

SOCIOLOGIC NEEDS. The continuing couple relationship allows easy fulfillment of society's rule that people be grouped two by two. The single individual is often urged to bring a date, dinner partner, or other "mate" to avoid his or her being a single at a social function. All singles activities—weekends, cruises, clubs—use the lure that by joining you may meet your "mate."

Although society today recognizes the single state as meaningful and even creditworthy, family members and peer groups still often urge the 30-year-old bachelor or career women to settle down and start raising a family. And there is a feeling of ambivalence about the presence of a recent divorcee at a couple event. The lone person is a threat in a society composed of couples, and will soon find himself in a social solitude until he rejoins society as part of a couple.

ECONOMIC NEEDS. Through history economic needs have brought couples together. In primitive civilizations, couple or family unions were often necessary for economic survival; in a classic division of labor the man provided food and shelter, the woman cooked and sewed. As society has became more complex and affluent, and work depends less on physical labor, there is less economic necessity for couple relationships. Today's women are no longer chained to economic dependence on men; the modern man can and often does cook, wash, and clean, and need not rely upon the woman for these services. Nevertheless, the couple continues to be a valid system of economic interdependence, involving division of labor and cooperative effort, in both traditional and alternative couple categories.

In business, particularly, it is often advantageous for two individuals to join forces, perhaps for monetary investment, sharing of a workload, or division of responsibility. What one cannot do alone can often be accomplished by two.

VARIATIONS IN NEEDS. These four types of needs may be actual or perceived, essential or unessential, absolute or relative, inherent or learned. Needs are often learned from role models, and thus in families in which close companionship, intellectual prowess, or physical attractiveness is prized, offspring will have perceived needs for these same attributes in a prospective partner. Daughters of strong fathers tend to seek strong mates, if the father-daughter relationship has been good.

Needs change during the individual's life cycle. The infant needs the nurturing care of the mother, while the young child requires the economic support of parents and the socializing influences of adult role models. Adolescents and young adults strive for psychologic validation of their attractiveness and self-worth and eventually for biologic gratification of their sexual urges. During mid-life, economic needs may come to the fore and the mid-life crisis may cause an abrupt shift in psychologic needs.[21]   In later life the couple relationship may fill biologic needs for personal care, economic needs for financial independence, and sociologic and psychologic needs for companionship.[20]

Although all types of couple relationships fulfill individual needs to some degree, the four types of needs appear to be met most fully by the traditional relationship of husband and wife: The needs met are the access to biologic essentials of food, shelter, and sexual activity, the economic interdependence to support the family unit, the sociologic sanction of the union, and the psychologic needs for approval, security, and love.

Other couple categories fill some or all of the four basic couple needs. Roger and Gloria, employer and employee, found that their relationship brought economic stability, social approval from their customers, and psychologic validation of their self-worth. For widower Joseph and his daughter Maria, the couple alliance filled the father's needs for personal care, the daughter's need to maintain the least expensive living arrangements, and the psychologic needs of both for companionship. For George and Frank being a couple filled their biologic needs for sexual gratification, economic needs for living accommodations, and psychologic needs for emotional support. Charles and Michael lived together, socially accepted as roommates, for reasons of economic origin.

Fears

Fear of loss, of the unknown, and of change all help keep couples together. Fear of economic loss helped insure that John and Margaret would stay together. Margaret was unlikely to leave her new-found source of affluence and John realized that divorcing his new second wife would cost him dearly in alimony.

Fear of loneliness also keeps many couples close, and helped perpetuate the couple relationships of professor Phyllis and student Nancy, John and Margaret, and Lucille and her daughter Martha.

Fear of the unknown and of change is a strong unifying force, and one which becomes more potent with increasing years. Roger and Gloria settled into a couple relationship and the thought of change filled both with dread, as Roger could not bear the prospect of having to train a new waitress and Gloria could not imagine having another employer.

Support Systems

Couple relationships are bolstered by support systems, the most influential of which is the family. The opinions and actions of peers are important, as friends rally to stabilize a faltering relationship or may conspire to destroy a union viewed as harmful. The church has long lent stability to marital couples and families; professional help is available to couples through physicians and counselors.

A positive support system may tip the scales in favor of continuing a couple relationship. An outside opinion confirms the worth of the relationship. The couple cannot help but ponder the fact that if others think the union is good, then there must be some value to it. And couple partners will invariably assess their relationship in a more positive light when others lend support.

Inertia

A thrown ball will sail through its trajectory—unless it strikes a wall or some other object that abruptly stops its flight The Newtonian theory that a body in motion tends to remain in motion applies to the couple trajectory. Once formed, the couple entity tends to persist, a positive force that helps many couples survive major crises. The man and woman who have been together for 20 years assume that they will stay together and can focus their energy on solving a problem—such as delinquency, alcoholism, or prolonged illness—which might drive a casual couple apart.

By the same theory of inertia, a body at rest tends to remain at rest and many couple unions continue in a state of ennui or disinterested coexistence, persisting for no better reason than that no stress has been sufficient to bring the final split.

COUPLE FOCUS: CHAPTER THREE

1. What are the various types of couples?

2. Can you think of one couple you know in each of these categories?

3. In how many of these couple categories are you involved?

3

A T AGE 18 NANCY HAD PARENT-CHILD relationships with each of her parents and had recently ended a year-long romance with a hometown boyfriend. At college, she began a friendship with her dormitory roommate, had a brief and unhappy affair with a campus football hero, and eventually formed a homosexual couple alliance with her professor of literature.

At any time in life, a person may engage in several couple relationships, based on different needs and understandings (couple contracts) and projected to reach different levels of involvement and duration (couple trajectory). A newly married couple may focus on their relationship to the virtual exclusion of all others; yet the others exist. At the opposite end of the spectrum, a physician, teacher, or counselor may form many intense couple relationships in the course of daily professional life, and sometimes these may overshadow vital couple commitments at home.

We usually think of a couple as man and woman: sexually attracted to one another, courting, marrying, bearing and rearing offspring, and providing one another companionship and security during the later years. But the complex demands of modern society—division of labor, commerce, education, travel, health care, anxiety, and sexuality—have led to the evolution of alternative couple unions.

COUPLE CATEGORIES

A couple may be categorized according to whether the partners are of the opposite or same sex, the same or different generation, and whether they are involved in a sexual or asexual union. These three biological criteria are the most fundamental points of differentiation, and the characteristics of couples vary little with other criteria such as whether they live together or not, or engage in long or short-term relationships. The various combinations of these three basic criteria describe the eight couple categories shown in Table 1.

Couple Category I: Opposite Sex, Intragenerational, Sexual Relationship

The sexual relationship between a man and woman of similar ages is the prototype couple relationship that has survived since Adam and Eve.

The union may be as transitory as a single dance at a social function or as enduring as a marriage of 50 years duration. Inclusion in this category usually implies that sexual attraction is involved and that some courting and caring occurs. However, actual coital activity does not necessarily exist in all Category I couples.

This category includes couples who are dating, engaged, living together, or married. Variations include two persons flirting at a party, the elderly man and woman who see one another socially, and even the prostitute and her "John."

Couple Category II: Opposite Sex, Intragenerational, Asexual

Business or social activity is usually the basis for the Category II male-female relationship involving individuals of

TABLE 1: COUPLE CATEGORIES

Sex	Generation	Sexual	Category		Examples
Opposite	Same	Yes	I.	Opposite sex, Intra-generational, Sexual	Living together or married
		No	II.	Opposite sex, Intra-generational, Asexual	Similar age sister-brother
		Yes	III.	Opposite sex, Inter-generational, Sexual	Older man/younger woman or older woman/younger man
	Other	No	IV.	Opposite sex, Inter-generational, Asexual	Father/daughter or mother/son
Same	Same	Yes	V.	Same sex, Intra-generational, Sexual	Similar age man/man or woman/woman
		No	VI.	Same sex, Intra-generational, Asexual	Roommates
		Yes	VII.	Same sex, Inter-generational, Sexual	Older/younger man/man or woman/woman
	Other	No	VIII.	Same sex, Inter-generational, Asexual	Mother/daughter or father/son

similar age. Needs met are primarily economic and sociologic and the couple may or may not live together. Nevertheless, Category II couple relationships may be as lasting as Category I and, in fact, the individual who has both a married couple relationship with one person and a business relationship with another may find it easier to end the marriage by divorce than to risk financial loss by breaking a contract.

There may be Category II relationships between siblings for cohabitation, social convenience, or business activity, and sexuality is prohibited by the incest taboo.

Among the various types of opposite sex, intragenerational, asexual couples are employer and employees or co-workers of the opposite sex, such as executive and secretary, partners in a business venture, manager and worker, or instructors in two-person teaching teams. Category II couples may be collaborators on a project—co-chairpersons of a committee, two writers working on a play, or two classmates working on a report. Or they may be partners in a social activity such as singers in a duet, male and female leads in a play, or opponents in a game of chess.

The absence of sexual activity does not preclude a meaningful couple relationship, as the following couple story shows:

Roger and Gloria: Roger was a 57-year-old owner of a small corner restaurant. His day began early as he welcomed breakfast customers on their way to work. The pace slowed in midmorning only to quicken at noon as the lunch customers arrived. The dinner crowd was more sparse and the last person usually finished his meal by 8 p.m.

Gloria, age 58, had worked with Roger for 16 years. She usually arrived after Roger in the morning but stayed until the last dish and glass were washed each evening. Through the years they had become an effective team, with Roger managing the food and ordering supplies while Gloria waited tables and collected cash from the customers.

Beyond their work together, they cared about one another: Gloria insisted that she prepare Roger's meals for him, seeing that he had ample time to enjoy his food even if customers waited. On balance, Roger assured Gloria's safe arrival home after work and helped with small repairs at her house.

The main focus of Roger's life was his restaurant and the livelihood it provided. He looked forward each year to his three-week Florida vacation and dreamed of the day when he could retire there permanently. Gloria's chief interest was in church activities; she taught a Sunday school class, attended worship service, and returned for a discussion group each Sunday evening. Both were oblivious to their relationship and would have laughed in embarrassment had anyone called them a couple.

Couple Category III: Opposite Sex, Intergenerational, Sexual Relationship

This couple category shares many features with Couple Category I, but with the significant difference that Category III couples are not of the same generation. These so-called May-December relationships, although ostensibly sexual, are often based on other than sexual needs.[24] For the older partner there is often the biological need for care in time of actual or anticipated illness, or for assurance of food, shelter, or physical comfort. The older partner also receives psychological affirmation of his or her desirability. In turn, the younger partner often has needs for wealth, opportunity, or emotional security. The affair between a middle-aged housewife and delivery boy brings her reassurance of continued attractiveness and him a safe opportunity for sexual self-expression.

Examples of Category III Opposite Sex, Intergenerational, Sexual Relationships include the older man-younger woman or the older woman-younger man who are dating, engaged, living together, or married. With one partner in the middle years or beyond, the decision to live together or to marry may be colored by economic considerations such as alimony or social security payments. If the generational difference is considerable, advancing years may see the sexual urge of the older partner wane, yet the sexual basis of the relationship persists and the couple remains in Category III.

> *John and Margaret:* When Margaret let her husband following four years of a childless marriage, she vowed, "Next time I'm going to do better."
>
> Upon eloping with her childhood sweetheart at age 18, Margaret soon found that married life was not the "happily ever after" that she had imagined. On her husband's modest salary as a steelworker, she wore last year's fashions and drove a Ford with a dented fender; and she wished for better. Rather than discuss their differences, he spent his evenings playing sports and drinking at a bar with "the boys." There soon developed a schism that would never be bridged.
>
> John's divorce came later in life. After a 25-year career spent climbing the executive ladder, John reached vice-presidency and his mid-life crises simultaneously. He reassessed his job, his marriage and his life, and found them wanting. At age 50, without a clear idea of where he

was headed, he escaped from his first marriage and the organizational hierarchy to begin his own small electronics business. With his training and experience, as well as the renewed vitality of middle age, John saw his new business prosper. By age 53 his income exceeded his previous corporate salary; yet John felt that life had more to offer.

John and Margaret met on a vacation in the Caribbean and married after a six-week courtship. Although their individual needs were never verbalized to one another, each was clearly defined. For Margaret, the union brought the affluence and social opportunities denied her in her first marriage. For John the marriage filled the mid-life fantasies of youthfulness, glamour, and sexuality.

Couple Category IV: Opposite Sex, Intergenerational, Asexual Relationship

Category IV couples may form within or outside family bonds. The relationship is similar to Category II except for the generational difference, and the union may be based on economic or social needs. Category IV, Opposite Sex, Intergenerational, Asexual Relationships include family couples such as father-daughter, mother-son, aunt-nephew, uncle-niece, and grandparent-grandchild. Other examples are employer-employee or co-workers of different generations such as executive-secretary, partners in a business venture, shopkeeper-clerk, or two teachers working together. The individuals may be collaborators on a project such as a school dance, a book, or a community program; they may be partners in an activity such as dancers in a pas de deux, male-female lead in a play, or mixed doubles tennis team. A common Category IV couple relationship is the opposite sex teacher and pupil.

Needs filled by Category IV couple relationships vary according to the ages of the partners. The parent-child relationship between a youngster and mother or father fills the dependency needs of the child and the parenting needs of the adult. When the parent-child relationship involves the middle and older generations, the couple relationship may fill biologic needs of the older parent, psychologic needs of the middle-aged child, and the economic needs of both. Extra-familial Category IV relationships are usually based on business and social needs.

Couple Category V: Same Sex,
Intragenerational, Sexual Relationship

This couple category describes the union of two partners of like ages engaging in the same-sex sexual relationship. The couple may or may not live together and the duration of the couple relationship may be brief or lasting. Examples include the male-male homosexual and the female-female Lesbian relationships.

The Category V relationship fills the biologic needs for the homosexual sexual experience. Economic needs may be met if the couple lives together and may be all-important if one partner is a professional prostitute. Sociologic needs for peer approval may be met within the homosexual community; on the other hand, the homosexual couple union may encounter social rejection with the "straight" community. The Category V relationship meets the special psychological needs of the homosexual individual, bringing this person tenderness, companionship, and love.

Couple Category VI: Same Sex, Intragenerational, Asexual Relationship

Two individuals of the same sex may form an asexual couple relationship for a variety of reasons including cohabitation, travel, business, or social needs. The affiliation may be voluntary or may be mandated, as in the case of roommates on a trip or cellmates in prison. In a Category VI relationship, the contract between the participants is often for the duration of a specified activity such as a trip duration or jail term. Other Category VI couples include colleagues or collaborators such as partners in business or profession, co-captains of a team, co-stars in a play, running mates in an election, or a two-man truck driver team.

Charles and Michael: Charles and Michael, both in their late teens and freshmen at the State University, were assigned as roommates by the Dean of Housing. They met for the first time in the room they were to share for the year.

Charles was the eldest son of a successful businessman. Father and son shared interests in golf and tennis and the relationship within the family was best described as tolerant and lenient. His tuition was paid by his father and supplemented by Charles' participation as lead guitar player in a rock band. The 50-mile move to the university prohibited Charles from attending weeknight practice with the group, but allowed him to participate in weekend performances.

Michael was the third son of a farm family and since childhood had been imbued with high academic aspirations. He planned to become a chemical engineer and crammed his schedule with mathematics and science courses, with full morning classes and afternoon laboratories. Evenings were devoted to study in preparation for the next day's classes. Charles' academic ambitions were less lofty and he viewed college as a pleasurable interlude between high school graduation and the time he would enter his father's hardware business.

The boys flipped a coin to decide the choice of bed and desk, and pooled funds to buy an easy chair and floor lamp for the room. Michael posed no threat to Charles' modest scholastic endeavors and active social life, while Charles' frequent absence from the room allowed Michael the uninterrupted study time he needed. The couple seemed compatible, at least at first.

Couple Category VII: Same Sex, Intergenerational, Sexual Relationship

Of all relationships, the Category VII relationship is the least socially sanctioned. There is often a presumption of exploitation, although a mutual need may be involved. Examples of the Category VII Same Sex, Intergenerational, Sexual Relationship include the male-male homosexual and the female-female Lesbian unions between child and adult or between two adults of different stages in the individual life cycle. The couple may or may not live together, may involve some economic gain (as in the prostitute-client relationship) or none, and may in fact include some degree of coercion. Involvement may be as fragile as an hour's liaison or as durable as the relationship described next.

Phyllis and Nancy: At age 48, Phyllis felt secure in her role as Associate Professor of English Literature at Western State University. She was generally liked by students and her courses filled early and were often overcrowded as late registrants implored her to accept them into her class. Phyllis usually said yes and her relationship with her students was, on the whole, more personal than that of most other professors.

Nancy entered the university at age 18. Her second semester course with Phyllis prompted her to change her major from American history to literature and the bonds between these two individuals grew over the next four years.

Writing was an important aspect of their relationship. In the beginning, Phyllis wrote long critiques of Nancy's class assignments, praising her insight and sensitivity. In response, Nancy wrote a short personal note to Phyllis which was answered with a longer letter and an invitation to tea. Their correspondence evolved into a weekly exchange of long letters covering virtually every aspect of human existence and during their increasingly frequent meetings, the two women discussed their feelings concerning the topics of their writing.

As they explored more deeply into the fiber of each other's being, a sense of intimacy arose, eventually developing into an ongoing sexual relationship during Nancy's senior year. For the sake of propriety, Nancy continued living in her dormitory room and Phyllis continued to live in her three-room downtown apartment. Weekends were spent together in the apartment, where they sipped wine, discussed music, art, and literature, and made love.

Couple Category VIII: Same Sex, Intergenerational, Asexual Relationship

The Category VIII relationship involves two individuals of the same sex, yet different generations, who unite for reasons including living arrangements, business endeavors, or social activities, and who may or may not live together. There may be family ties: mother-daughter, father-son, aunt-niece, uncle-nephew, grandmother-granddaughter, grandfather-grandson. Other Category VIII couples may be teacher-student, coach-athlete, employer-employee, or co-workers, including business partners, a two-man truck driver team, a two-person police team, or beauticians in a two-person ship—all involving an older and a younger partner.

The Category VIII couple may meet biological needs of food and shelter when the couple live together. More pertinent are economic and psychosocial needs, and Category VIII couples have many similarities with Categories II, IV, and VI couples.

OTHER COUPLE RELATIONSHIPS

The couple concept can be expanded to include relationships other than those between two individuals. One example would be the couple union between a priest or nun and the Roman Catholic Church, including the tradition that the nun wear a wedding ring. More extreme relationships might include the man who is "wedded to his work," the individual whose most meaningful interaction is with a pet dog or cat, or the zealot who forsakes family and friends in favor of a cause. Literary examples of heroes who form couple relationships with beasts, elements of nature, or supernatural beings include Benet's *The Devil and Daniel Webster* and Hemingway's *The Old Man and the Sea.*

COUPLE FOCUS: CHAPTER FOUR

1. What are the levels at which couple partners interact?

2. At what interaction level is each of your couple relationships?

3. Why are couple interactions not always what they seem to be on the surface?

4. What are the benefits and risks of deeper couple interactions?

4

W E KNOW SOME COUPLES who seem as close as riders on a rush-hour subway; they anticipate each other's needs and one almost appears to know what the other is thinking. Other couples seem oblivious to each other as they hurry in opposite directions; they have been called "married singles."[5]

Every couple interacts at a specific level. Analyzing the way two individuals relate to each other helps determine a couple's likelihood of staying together or separating. The level of interaction is determined initially by the contract negotiated. The Category VI couple who contract to share an apartment for convenience do so for chiefly economic needs; their contract is at a superficial level of interaction and they aspire to a limited interpersonal involvement. By contrast, the Category I married couple will fulfill more intimate biologic and psychologic needs; they contract for a deeper level of interaction and aim for higher degrees of involvement.

COUPLE INTERACTIONS

We have found that couple partners relate to each other at one of four levels—(1) convenience, (2) supportive, (3) nurturative, and (4) unitive—identified by the degree to which individual and couple needs are met.

No couple category has a monopoly on any one level of interaction and, in fact, a couple in any category can interact at any level. Thus the relationship between roommates Charles and Michael—clearly an interaction of convenience—could eventually progress to a supportive, nurturative, or even unitive relationship.

Level 1: Interaction of Convenience

This most superficial level of interaction is found when the couple's needs and goals focus on objects and activities. The distinguishing feature of this interaction is that if fills a need—often only a single neeed—which is met in a convenient manner without consideration of other aspects of the relationship.

Many couples have Convenience Interactions: The transient relationship between prostitute and customer fills the customer's "need" for release of sexual tension and the prostitute's need for continuing income. "Blind date" dinner partners at a social function fill their social needs for an evening's participation as a couple and the individuals feel under no obligation to meet in the future. An arranged marriage to gain citizenship for one partner is a Convenience Interaction and fills a social and economic need; the couple interaction may or may not mature to a deeper level. Two strangers who turn to one another for emotional support in time of crisis fill a transient psychologic need, and do so without further commitment.

Category II (Opposite Sex, Intragenerational, Asexual) couples often function at interactions of convenience. The focus is on economic and social needs: filling job roles and earning a living in a socially approved manner. For example, a young man and woman working side by side in a busy office may maintain a Convenience Interaction for many years. Similar examples can be drawn from all seven other couple categories and might include cellmates in a prison, assigned roommates in a dormitory or cruise ship, riders on an amusement park roller coaster, or random sharers of any two-person conveyance or activity.

Joseph and Maria: Joseph, his wife, and their daughter Maria came to America from Italy 23 years ago. After growing up and reaching adulthood in her new homeland, Maria left her parents' inner city home and found a secretarial job in a suburban manufacturing company. She took an apartment near her job where she lived alone, dating occasionally, and spending most of her evenings and weekends reading and watching television. When Maria was 29, her mother died. Her father, Joseph, had spent his American years working in a warehouse with other Italians and had learned only a few words of English. His wife's death left him with a desperate feeling of isolation. He sought help from his family physician who prescribed medication and who called Maria, suggesting that she stay with her father during his time of emotional upheaval.

Maria persuaded Joseph to give up the apartment that he and her mother had shared and to move into the spare bedroom in her own apartment. With mixed feelings, Joseph agreed and for seven years he and his daughter lived together.

After the first six months Joseph's depression passed and he soon re-established friendships with his cronies, who visited the apartment frequently. Her previously quiet life now subject to evening interruptions, Maria began to take more interest in neighborhood and church events.

Filial devotion prevented Maria from expressing or even contemplating disapproval of her father's presence. The father, on the other hand, seemed aware that he intruded on Maria's life; yet he lacked the money and initiative to make a change. Together they evolved a couple relationship which both continued to consider temporary even though it had persisted for seven years. Maria provided the bulk of the family income, which was supplemented by Joseph's pension. Joseph did most of the shopping, cooking, and cleaning. Yet they led separate lives and interacted only on a surface level.

Although they were father and daughter, Joseph and Maria lived together as roommates, traveling companions through life. The couple relationship met biologic needs for food and shelter and offered the economic advantages of a single household. The father-daughter life together met with general societal approval. However, psychological benefits of the relationship were minimal and, in fact, were probably overshadowed by Maria's altered lifestyle and Joseph's feelings of dependence.

Level 2: Supportive Interaction

The Supportive Interaction meets convenience needs of the partners and also offers personal support for their activities and endeavors. The supportive relationship involves a deeper level of interaction and the couple trajectory shows a greater personal involvement in the couple relationship. There is approval of one another's lifestyles, endeavors, and goals, and a willingness to render aid and comfort when needed.

The focus of Level 2 Supportive Interactions is on economic and sociologic activities. For example, in the intergenerational marriage of John and Margaret, she supported his economic endeavors while he encouraged her quest for beauty and fashion.

Supportive interactions are common in intragenerational, asexual couples (Categories II and IV): individuals sharing a room or apartment, co-workers in a continuing relationship, collaborators on a project, employer and employee of the same age, and teammates working for a common goal.

A common example of supportive couple interaction is found in the Category VIII couple: family members of the same sex and different generations who seek out one another following loss or death of previous couple partners.

Lucille and Martha: Martha forgave her husband's alcoholic bouts and physical abuse for 14 years, staying with him for the sake of the three children. The final break came when he broke her jaw during a drunken rage. While Martha was in the hospital, the children were cared for by their maternal grandmother, Lucille. After discharge from the hospital, Martha joined the children at her mother's home and filed for divorce.

During the next five years the two women formed a supportive couple relationship, and shared the task of raising three youngsters.

Lucille, living on a widow's pension, welcomed Martha and her children into her home and their presence filled a lonely void. Martha became wage earner, and Lucille kept house for the family. Outside the home, Lucille continued to be active in church and volunteer services, while Martha joined the bowling team in her company-sponsored league. Each encouraged the other in outside activities and in their roles within the family.

Lucille and Martha developed a distinct couple relationship, with mutual support of economic and social endeavors. There was cooperation in meeting biological needs for food and shelter and the relationship filled psychologic needs for companionship. Nevertheless, both Lucille and Martha considered the relationship to be temporary. Following her divorce, Martha dated from time to time, and both she and her mother conceded that the family life would probably be altered as the youngsters left home or if Martha remarried.

Level 3: Nurturative Interaction

The Level 3 Nurturative Interaction meets the needs for convenience and support of previous levels but adds the important ingredient of active caring and involvement in the well-being of the partner. At this level of interaction there is an increased sense of commitment and closeness, and a greater presumption of remaining together. Role definition is greater and there is a heightened awareness of one another's values and feelings. Each partner participates with the other in developing deeper levels of personal growth and understanding.

Although sexual activity occurs at all levels of interaction, couple categories involving sexual relationships (Categories I, III, V, and VII) report that sex is most meaningful at this and the following level of interaction.

Of course, sexual activity (and Nurturative Interactions) are not limited to heterosexual couples.

George and Frank: Frank was the youngest of five children, the long-awaited son following four daughters.

His father, who had been a high school halfback in his youth, had dreamed of having a strong, aggressive son through whom he could vicariously relive his days of athletic glory. By Frank's 10th birthday, it was apparent that the frail and gentle lad lacked the aggressiveness to win at sports and was headed for a life of quiet scholarship. At this time, Frank's father left home, leaving the boy the only male in a house of women and the subject of their solicitous attention. Through high school and his three years of Army duty, Frank seldom dated. At age 25 he became infatuated with a 17-year-old high school student. Following a few dates that lasted until early morning hours, they ran away and married. Within a year a son was born and three months later, Frank's wife and son deserted him. Following this loss, Frank turned for comfort to his long-time acquaintance, George.

George was the youngest son of a couple who freely admitted that George was a late-in-life mistake. Both parents took pride in their corner grocery store and the mom-and-pop business was clearly dominated by George's mother, who bullied his father into submission on every issue. As he reached school age, George was generally left to fix his own meals, keep the house, and plan his life as his parents purchased supplies and ran their business.

At 18 George left home, much to the relief of his parents with whom he maintained little contact during the years that followed.

During his teenage years, George had had furtive liaisons with both girls and boys. He soon concluded that his female lovers were fickle and threatening while male lovers were more loyal and comfortable. By his early 20's George was a confirmed homosexual, engaging in a series of more or less continuing relationships punctuated by sporadic interludes with individuals met at gay bars. Yet George maintained a job, and he kept his career and homosexual lives separate. By his late 20's the strain of his double life was becoming onerous and George had decided that the time had come to proclaim his homosexuality. It was at this time that he began a relationship with the distraught Frank. Their commiseration progressed to physical intimacy and a subsequent commitment to live together.

For the following 18 years George and Frank shared a small house. They carefully avoided the stereotyped roles of the homosexual; both remained employed and they shared household duties. But neither dated and each remained sexually faithful to the other. To be sure, they had divergent intellectual interests and each reflected the antithesis of his parents. Frank remained the bespectacled reader while George attended dance classes and theatre rehearsals. Yet they helped one another in times of need and when George was hospitalized for possible intestinal obstruction, Frank's concern was apparent and real.

During their years together George and Frank evolved a Nurturative Interaction. Each supported the lifestyle, endeavors, and personal growth of the other and there was an active concern for one another's well-being.

Level 4: Unitive Interaction

The deepest level of interaction is called unitive, and involves a profound commitment to the couple relationship with a tacit understanding that the couple is of greater value than the two partners. There is an intimacy unattained in Levels

1, 2, and 3, with an open expression of thoughts, emotions, and feelings. The couple contract and trajectory reflect intense involvement of long duration.

The Unitive Interaction evolves as the couple passes progressively through the previous three stages. Most couples fall short of the unitive stage of interaction and their development is arrested at a lower level. Those who reach the unitive level may do so by unintentional evolution of the relationship or by studied design. The former is the case in most instances and the sense of true couple unity develops gradually—and with much hard work—over months and years. Those couples who seek and attain a Unitive Interaction do so by regular use of communication techniques that help partners reveal inner emotions to one another and accept these emotions openly.[4,9,12]

Needs met by the unitive relationship include biologic, economic, and sociologic, but the focus is on psychologic. The couples achieving a Unitive Interaction enjoy full confidence in the relationship; the partners are offered maximum opportunity for individual and joint pursuit of life goals with assurance of nonjudgmental acceptance of feelings, actions, and outcomes.

Although this level of interaction can be achieved in all couple categories, we find it most commonly in the heterosexual relationships (Couple Categories I and III), those couples that are dating, engaged, living together, or married.

Harry and Jane: Harry and Jane were both in their mid-30's and had been married for 13 years. They grew up in nearby small towns, and dated from time to time during their teenage years. Following their respective high school graduations, Harry took a job at a plumbing supply distributor and Jane began work as a secretary. Both dated others during their early 20's, and gradually they narrowed their attention to one another. Their formal courtship lasted 18 months, followed by a large Catholic Church wedding attended by many members of both families.

The third year of marriage brought their first child, whose gestation and birth was noteworthy in that both parents studied and practiced the techniques of natural childbirth. Harry would say, "We try to do things together. Why should Jane have all the fun?"

Harry and Jane actively worked to build their couple relationship. They studied and discussed books, and wrote one another notes telling their thoughts about ideas in literature, television, and movies. They worked to make their marriage what they described as "better than most" and maintained a discipline of daily dialogue.

Harry and Jane continued to do things together: housework, yardwork, vacation planning, and child care. Their involvement with each other was intense and was consciously directed toward learning more and more about each other and toward improving their marriage.

INTERACTIONS AND THE COUPLE

Couples can move freely from one interaction level to another; mobility is generally to a deeper level of interaction, as the supportive couple begins to show active caring, or as the couple in a Nurturative Interaction begins open communication. Relationships usually begin at the level of convenience—the convenience of a shared table or blind date—and may or may not show progression. The deeper the level of couple interaction, the higher and longer the couple trajectory and the deeper the likelihood of couple continuation, even in times of stress.

Couple interactions may not always be what they seem on the surface. To the casual observer, John and Margaret may have appeared to have a Nurturative Interaction; yet their interaction level was at best supportive and perhaps only one of convenience. Maria and her father, Joseph, had an interaction of convenience and their progression to a deeper level was largely prohibited by the agreement that their sharing the same roof was a temporary arrangement. To casual acquaintances George and Frank may have appeared to be living together for convenience when in fact their relationship was highly nurturative and could have become unitive if each had sought full involvement in their "marriage."

Benefits and Risks

Any couple interaction carries the promise of benefits and the threat of personal risks. As a relationship deepens, both the benefits and risks tend to increase. Each participant consciously or unconsciously weighs these possibilities in balance, and the benefit: risk ratio is evaluated by each partner before a couple moves from one interaction level to the next. One couple partner may be ready for a deeper interaction; the other may fear the risks, and a joint shift in interaction will await mutual agreement. Jane sometimes recalled her dating days when she was ready to be engaged but Harry, who was not ready yet, would change the subject.

The Level 1 Convenience Interaction involves scant personal investment of effort, emotions, or identity. The implied transitory nature of the relationship and the superficial interaction make this a low-risk investment. Classmates and teammates separate without remorse, and never seek out one another again. Accordingly, the benefits derived are the lowest of all interaction levels.

The benefits of the Level 2 Supportive and Level 3 Nurturative Interactions are greater, offering greater physical and emotional support and subsequently interpersonal involvement and caring. Lucille and Martha, as well as George and Frank, enjoy a closeness based on trust and caring. Accordingly, the personal risks to self are increased as involvement becomes progressively invested in the relationship.

The greatest potential benefits and risks lie in the Level 4 Unitive Interaction wherein maximum commitment is made to the couple relationship. The benefits derived are total approval and acceptance of self with the opportunities for full honesty within the relationship. On balance, the full emotional investment in the relationship carries the risk of total loss if a couple such as Jane and Harry meets death, separation, desertion, divorce, or other unplanned end.

EFFECT ON COUPLE STABILITY

The four levels of interaction help us determine couple stability. For each couple studies the probability of couple continuation increases arithmetically as the level of couple interaction progresses. Couple Stability Index Values are assigned to the four interaction levels as follows:

Level of Interaction	Couple Stability Index Value
Convenience	+1
Supportive	+2
Nurturative	+3
Unitive	+4

**COUPLE
FOCUS:
CHAPTER
FIVE**

1. What are the stages of the couple
   life cycle?

2. In what stage is each of your
   couple relationships?

3. How can a person pass through
   the couple life cycle more than
   once?

4. How does the stage of the couple
   life cycle influence couple stability?

5

JANE AND HARRY FACED a crisis during their sixth year of marriage. Jane felt unfulfilled; Harry felt trapped; both decided that they had little in common except the children and a mortgage. They alternately bickered and pouted, and even discussed divorce.

A family friend guided the couple to a marriage counselor, who helped them examine their feelings about themselves, each other, and their marriage. Eventually they came to understand their apparent conflict as a stage in couple life when the relationship is re-evaluated. Jane and Harry's period of couple assessment coincided with changes in their own personal life cycles and their family life cycle, compounding the stress on the relationship.

A person passes through six sequential stages of life: infancy, childhood, adolescence, young adulthood, middle age, and old age. Each builds on the previous phases, and a person passes through these stages only once. Within each stage the individual faces characteristic stresses—such as beginning school, marriage, job change, retirement—which can be anticipated and, it is hoped, handled in a positive manner. Knowing a person's life stage helps predict the problems he may face, both at that stage and in his or her passage to the next.[18]

For those individuals who form a parenting relationship, there are also family life stages. The couple family becomes a parenting family, first with preschool, then schoolage, and eventually teenage children. Once the children are launched, the couple are again the family, entering the post-parental and later the retirement years. We each pass through life but once, yet we may experience family life stages several times. A person may experience one or more of the family life stages, then leave that family and enter into another family life cycle at the beginning or at a different level. Just as the transition between two life stages—for example, from childhood to adolescence—may be turbulent, the shifts from family parenting to launching to post-parenting and retirement may be tumultuous.

Couples too pass through sequential stages, differing from individual and family life cycles in that they reflect the one-to-one relationship. The couple becomes an entity as real as a person or family, and the couple life cycle is separate and distinct from the life stages of its two partners.

STAGES OF COUPLE LIFE

The couple life cycle is divided into four stages: (1) commitment, (2) accommodation, (3) assessment, and (4) recommitment (or termination). Each stage of the couple life cycle has its own special characteristics which affect the couple (see Table 2).

Stage 1: Commitment

The Commitment Stage of a couple relationship begins with the initial pact to function as a twosome, whether the agreement is for a brief or long-term relationship. Couple commitment may begin with the agreement to meet for a date,

Stage in the Couple Life Cycle

Facet of Relationships	Commitment	Accommodation	Assessment	Recommitment
Individual tasks	Altering lifestyle and priorities by commitment to the couple relationship	Adjusting to partner's habits, idiosyncrasies, and faults	Inventory and Evaluation of current life status and options for the future	Restabilization of lifestyle and priorities
Individual approval needs	Confirmation of personal worth	Acceptance of habits, idiosyncrasies, and faults by partner	Self-validation of couple worth	Reconfirmation that the partner cares
Couple tasks	Establishing congruent life styles and priorities	Establishing common interests and goals	Maintaining sense of couple unity while re-evaluating individual status and goals	Rediscovering congruent life-styles and priorities
Couple approval needs	Approval from family	Approval from peer group	Approval from family and peer group	Self-approval of couple worth
Intimacy	Insecure and tenuous intimacy	Deepening but with periodic ambivalence	Threatened intimacy	Secure intimacy
Autonomy	Sharp reduction in individual autonomy	Early testing of autonomy limits	Rising desire for individual autonomy	Acceptance of realistic limits of autonomy
Sources of conflict	Old ties and lifestyle	Demands of new relationship	Questioning couple worth	Forces external to the couple
Dominance	Vying for dominance within the relationship	Establishing domains of power within the relationship	Questioning of dominance within the relationship	Establishment of modified patterns of dominance.

become engaged, or to marry. Or it might involve living together and sharing an apartment, dormitory room, or hotel room. It might also concern a joint effort such as a committee, play, partnership, or other socio-economic activity.

It is during the Commitment Stage that couple contracts are formed. The expressed contracts of the Commitment Stage identify the needs of each partner to be met by the other and by the couple relationship. The formal partnership agreement will outline the anticipated input and benefits of two businessmen; the marriage contract spells out the marital covenant; the commitment phase of apartment-sharing denotes what is expected of each participant.

Implied commitment contracts are less specific, and one or both partners may have unrealistic expectations. For example, the young woman accepting a blind date may believe she has contracted for dinner, theater, and perhaps a goodnight kiss. The male partner, on the other hand, may consider that the evening is just beginning when he returns his date to her apartment.

Sometimes the Commitment Stage involves a tradeoff by which couple partners meet specific needs:

John and Margaret. Both survivors of previous marital disasters, John and Margaret began their new marriage with memories of the past and hopes for the future. John's first marriage lasted 23 years, eventually dissolving during his mid-life crises. Margaret's teenage marriage brought neither joy nor material gain, and no tears were shed at the union's demise.

Although their ages differed by a generation, John and Margaret contracted a union that seemed to meet their current needs. Middle age begins when you awaken one morning with the realization that there are a finite number of years left, and John at 50 met this challenge by affecting a youthful lifestyle, including growing a beard, taking up jogging, and deserting the family that symbolized his age and obligations. His new self-image called for a youthful consort, with priority given to glamour rather than common sense, and to spontaneity rather than steadfastness.

Margaret's first husband had worked with his hands, and she vowed that her next marriage would be to a man who came home with clean fingernails—and with a salary that would allow charge accounts in the exclusive shops, her own sports car, and vacations to exotic places around the world. An age difference was unimportant, as long as the union could fulfill her material desires.

Thus these two previously married and divorced individuals of different ages began a commitment to a long-term couple relationship based upon a formal contract of marriage. Their immediate needs were identified and they entered into an implied contract to meet them. Specifically, Margaret fulfilled John's middle-aged needs for a young wife, an active social life, and vigorous sexual activity. On balance, John fulfilled Margaret's needs for affluence, travel, and status.

For good reason, the Commitment Stage of the couple life cycle may be called the "honeymoon." Conflicting needs are not yet totally apparent and there has been scant time for disagreements to develop. Thus the stability of couples in the Commitment Stage is great, and they are sure their unions will last forever.

Stage 2: Accommodation

Then the honeymoon is over. The couple bond weakens a little during the second stage of the couple life cycle. The stage of accommodation may be called "the period of adjustment," and it is here that differences arise. John discovered that Margaret's beauty necessitated an hour at the dressing table mirror each morning and visits to the beauty parlor three times weekly; Margaret learned that John's affluence was tempered by a touch of stinginess.

During the Accommodation Stage there lingers the idealism of commitment and each partner attempts to adapt to new needs, stresses, and annoyances as they arise. Disagreements may concern mundane topics such as who will shower first in the morning or more serious issues such as which partner will be the major income provider. Frequent negotiations are needed to make the alliance work.

Because new stresses are arising, the couple stability of Stage 2 is less than in Stage 1, as seen in the conflict that arose between roommates:

> *Charles and Michael:* Two college roommates are a couple—the association meeting a housing need and continuing through the school year—as surely as husband and wife.
>
> Following their assignment as roommates, Charles and Michael achieved a workable relationship in spite of differing personalities and goals. With a light liberal arts schedule, Charles was frequently absent from the dormitory, leaving Michael free to study for his more demanding engineering courses. When Charles returned each evening, he came bursting with tales of campus activities, allowing Michael to participate vicariously in the campus social life.

The stage of accommodation began as the first college marking period approached. Even Charles began to feel the academic pressure, and it became apparent that his social activities had precluded adequate scholastic effort. Charles' father warned him of the consequences of failure—clerking at the hardware store—and Charles resolved to take a greater interest in his studies. His shifting emphasis caused Charles to spend most evenings studying in the room, and Michael began to resent the intrusion upon his privacy. The couple conflict became worse when Michael discovered that Charles could study only to the sound of loud stereophonic music, while Michael could only concentrate in quiet surroundings.

Moreover, each boy discovered that the other had annoying habits. Charles was basically untidy, leaving underwear, socks, and books strewn about the room and tossing wastepaper haphazardly into a corner pile. Charles soon became irritated with Michael's long hours of evening quiet and his habit of noisy early morning rising.

Charles and Michael were in the Accommodation Stage. Each minor action of the other represented a stress on the relationship which might have been overlooked in the Commitment Stage. In Stage 1—Commitment—each person focuses on articulated and apparent needs. In the case of Charles and Michael this was the economic and social need to have a roommate in a dormitory. Once this need is satisfied, Stage 2—Accommodation—begins as initial presumptions concerning the partner and the couple relationship are validated or disproved. In the case of Charles and Michael, the seemingly compatible roommates turned out to have incompatible lifestyles.

Nevertheless, each partner makes adjustments and concessions throughout this stage in an effort to maintain the couple relationship for the duration of the contract. Charles turned his rock music to a slightly lower volume; Michael arose in the morning without slamming drawers and doors. They both realized that changing rooms prior to the end of the school year would be inconvenient and, at this stage of their association, they were willing to put up with each other's idiosyncrasies at least a little longer.

Stage 3: Assessment

During the third stage of the couple life cycle, the relationship is closely scrutinized and its worth carefully considered. The dreams of the Commitment Stage have faded and during the Accommodation Stage most of the partner's annoying habits, traits, and demands have been discovered.

Couple partners in Stage 3 may be undergoing simultaneous changes in their own personal life cycles and perhaps in their family life cycles. Personal life changes include the transitions from adolescence to young adulthood and more notably the shift to middle age. At these times, personal needs may arise which cannot be filled by the existing couple relationship: John needed a youthful companion to match his new lifestyle at age 50, a need that could not be met by his first wife.

The couple Assessment Stage may follow transitions in family life, particularly the changes from beginning to childbearing family, from parenting teenagers to launching them into the world, and from launching to the post-parental family. With the addition of the first child to the household comes a challenge to the husband-wife relationship, as mother and father each form a new couple bond with the infant. The shift from teenage parenting to launching involves granting of autonomy with changes in the parent-child interactions. Sharp disagreements often arise during this stage, and may lead to re-evaluation of the mother-father relationship.

Assessment of the marital couple relationship often occurs as children leave the home and previous need-filling parent-child bonds are broken. The emotional investment shifts from parenting to coupling, and there is renewed focus on the male-female middle age couple relationship. At this time, many persons in their 40's and 50's find that while raising a family and striving for personal advancement during the couple life stage of accommodation, they have grown apart without realizing the dichotomy. The departure of children and renewed attention concentrated on each other may make the disparity of interests, intellectual attainments, and personal needs all painfully apparent.

The Assessment Stage is the time when couple bonds are weakest. The marriage that would "last forever" may become a life sentence; infidelity, separation, and divorce may occur. Those couples who have deeper and more enduring interactions are more likely to have developed adaptive methods allowing them to weather the stresses; couples with more superficial and transitory relationships are more likely to see their alliances end at this time.

During the Assessment Stage the couple faces a conscious yes-no, go *vs.* no go decision concerning the relationship. Is the marriage—or other couple association—worth saving? If the couple survives the assessment and if it is decided that the benefits of the union outweigh the disadvantages, the couple relationship will continue and will progress to the Recommitment Stage. On the other hand, if one or both partners decide that woes exceed the joys, the couple relationship will end. A new relationship may begin between the two individuals, commonly expressed as "let's still be friends." A sexual relationship may terminate and an asexual association begin. Or alternatively, each may go his separate way and begin subsequent couple relationships with others, starting a new couple life cycle at the Commitment Stage.

Phyllis and Nancy: Phyllis and Nancy, the professor and student engaged in a Lesbian relationship, spent evenings and weekends in deep discussions, and wrote letters which allowed each to reveal inner emotions to the other. As trust developed over the four years of their association, they learned to accept each other's feelings, and they evolved an intense emotional as well as physical interaction as they passed through the couple life stages of commitment and accommodation.

The stage of assessment came with the realization that Nancy would graduate from college at the end of the current term. She would leave, probably to attend graduate school in a distant state. The certainty of separation prompted each to consider the course the relationship would take in the months and years to come. Should Nancy seek a graduate school closer to Phyllis? Should her plans for further education be aborted so that she could remain with Phyllis? Perhaps they could live together. Should Phyllis change her job to be closer to Nancy? Or should they be content to write and visit one another on weekends and holidays? Should the relationship be continued at all?

Harry and Jane: Harry and Jane weathered their stormy sixth year of marriage only to face a similar period of re-evaluation seven years later, as their last child entered school. Jane was dazzled by the new-found freedom of having both children in school all day, and Harry found the change and Jane's emerging aggressiveness threatening. What followed was an appraisal of their feelings about their children and each other. They spent long hours discussing their thoughts and emotions and used the problem solving techniques taught to them six years earlier. They negotiated what could be changed, acknowledged what could not, and accepted one another's feelings.

Stage 4: Recommitment

If the couple survives the stage of assessment and the decision is made to continue together, the Recommitment Stage begins. Of all stages in the couple life cycle, this is the most stable. Here is found a commitment to the relationship characteristic of Stage 1 plus a strong impetus to continue. The couple has survived the adjustments and concessions necessitated by the stage of accommodation, and the outcome of assessment has been a favorable appraisal of the union. Thus the two individuals have corrected or accepted each other's bad habits, passed judgement on the relationship, and found that it meets their needs.

Sometimes the four stages of the life cycle progress slowly and a couple reaches the stage of recommitment without being aware that anything has changed.

Roger and Gloria: Roger and Gloria made peace with Gloria's tendency to oversleep and arrive apologetically in the midst of the breakfast rush, and Roger's sleepy reluctance to converse until after his third cup of coffee.

Together they adjusted to the long grinding hours necessary to earn a living in a small restaurant, to the demands of customers, and to the lack of free time inherent in a service trade. They made their accommodation to the business and to each other. Roger ceased wondering if he should replace Gloria with a younger waitress who would arrive on time each morning and Gloria stopped wishing that her employer were less grumpy early in the day. Without being aware of it, they had individually taken inventory of the relationship, its drawbacks and benefits, and embarked upon a stage of recommitment.

Sometimes the decision is no, and the couple separates. When this happens, the couple life cycle is broken, and the Assessment Stage is followed by termination. There is separation, divorce, or other unplanned couple end, with the emotional wounds that such an event can cause.

PROGRESS THROUGH THE COUPLE LIFE CYCLE

All couples pass through the same life stages, some slowly and some rapidly. The dating couple may progress through all four stages within the space of a few evenings, culminating in either the shift to a deeper relationship or the termination of the union. For the couple who are married or living together, the progress may take months, years, or even decades. In the traditional husband-wife couple relationship, the Commitment Stage may begin in the late teens or early 20's and assessment may not be reached until the mid-life crises of one or both partners or the launching/post-parental transition in family life. The parent-child couple relationship usually does not reach the stage of assessment until the second decade of the child's life as the decision is made whether to remain together or for the child to leave to pursue new couple relationships.

As Harry and Jane did, any couple can pass through the couple life cycle more than once, and probably will. Each stage of recommitment establishes a couple contract which will be followed by accommodation, then assessment, and eventually another decision to continue or end the union.

EFFECT ON COUPLE STABILITY

The stages of the couple life cycle have important implications for couple stability, as these values indicate:

Stages in the Couple Life Cycle	Couple Stability Index Value
Commitment	+3
Accommodation	+2
Assessment	+1
Recommitment	+4

At all stages of the couple life cycle the inertia of the couple union gives a positive Couple Stability Index Value. The maximum of +4 is found during the Recommitment Stage. This is the time when the couple is most likely to overcome stress, with the traditional married couple (Category I) settling in for the long haul and other couple categories renewing their enthusiasm and dedication to the alliance.

The Commitment Stage (+3 Couple Stability Index Value) is slightly less likely to afford continuation. At this stage the couple has yet to weather the storms of accommodation and assessment, yet there is the starry-eyed agreement to give the relationship a fair try. It is noteworthy that the stability of the relationship is considered only for the duration of the contract and thus a commitment to be dinner partners may launch a full couple life cycle during fulfillment of the one evening contract of convenience.

With the Accommodation Stage comes a greater likelihood of termination and a +2 Couple Stability Index Value. Annoying faults are becoming apparent, and adaptive mechanisms may fail to avert a crisis.

During the Assessment Stage the likelihood of couple continuity is at its ebb. This time of maximum stress on the union is ascribed a +1 Couple Stability Index Value, which derives largely from the inertia of the relationship and fears of loss if termination occurs. Stresses of all types occur here and the use of adaptive methods becomes vital.

Recognizing where a couple is in its life cycle helps predict how firm the union will be if subjected to stress. The May-December marriage of John and Margaret was likely to survive its stage of commitment—at least until the honeymoon was over. The Charles-Michael roommate relationship was in greater jeopardy, as the two boys discovered more areas of disagreement. At greatest risk are couples in the Assessment Stage of couple life, where Harry and Jane were when they faced crisis for the second time.

The couples most likely to endure—and to survive the stresses of life—are those in the Recommitment Stage. Harry and Jane experienced their interpersonal problems and worked together to conquer them. The decision to continue—to enter Stage 4 of couple life—strengthened the bonds of their relationship.

COUPLE FOCUS: CHAPTER SIX

1. What types of stresses do couples face?

2. What stresses threaten your couple relationships at this time?

3. How does a person's or couple's value orientation influence the impact of stress?

6

WHAT DRIVES COUPLES APART? Why might a couple stay together through one crisis and later separate when a different stress is faced? Why might the same problem cause one couple to separate and another to grow closer?

STRESSES AND THE COUPLE RELATIONSHIP

Individuals, families, and couples face stress every day. For the individual there are the daily stresses of work, social interaction, and survival in a competitive world. The family faces the responses of its members to individual stresses plus such family crises as moving to a new home, job loss or disability of a major wage-earner, or major conflicts between members. Stresses faced by couples have certain similarities to those encountered by individuals and families, yet differ in that the stress involves two persons who may act in concert or in opposition.

Individual Stress

Individual stresses can be studied according to needs met by the couple relationship. Biologic stress may involve hunger, exposure, sexual deprivation, injury, or illness. Economic problems may concern occupational or financial failure, or even success. Sociologic stress encompasses a broad group of situations involving disapproval, isolation, or alienation. Most threatening of all to the individual may be psychologic stress, causing anxiety, guilt, fear, depression, or despair. Each of these individual stresses may strike one or more members of the couple and may be reflected as couple stress.

Family Stress

The family also experiences stress. Hill identifies four major categories of family crises: (1) *abandonment* may occur with the death of a child or spouse, or when a family member is in the hospital or off to war, (2) *addition*, such as the entry of a new member into the household, may upset the balance of intimacy and dominance within the household, (3) *demoralization*, including adultery, alcoholism, drug abuse, or delinquency, are common family problems, and (4) *status shifts*, including prolonged unemployment or sudden changes in family financial status, cause adjustments in family roles.[5]

Couple Stress

Individual or family stress may cause a couple crisis. The origin of stress may arise externally as in a distant job offer or accidental injury, or may occur as an internal catastrophe such as infidelity or drug abuse.[7] Stress affecting the individual threatens his physical and emotional well-being while family stress jeopardizes both the individual and the solidarity of his family.

Couple stress involves the individual, his or her nuclear and extended family, and most specifically the relationship between two human beings.

TYPES OF COUPLE STRESS

Our observations of couples have revealed definite patterns of couple stress. Conflicts arise concerning having, doing, relating, and being: that is, stresses on the couple relationship may occur in regard to (1) *objects*, (2) *activities*, (3) *values, roles, and extra-couple relationships,* and (4) *couple unity.*

Within each of these four categories it helps to think of those stresses which are ordinary and those which are extraordinary. Ordinary stresses are those generally expected to occur at one time or another in any couple relationship and include mundane decisions about buying or selling items, significant failure or success in personal endeavors, and normal shifts in personal and family life stages. One expects that the need to sell a home will produce stress, as will the loss of a desired promotion or the decisions facing the young couple living away from home for the first time.

Extraordinary stresses are those nor normally found in day-to-day life, yet when faced by couples are noteworthy causes of couple crises. Extraordinary stresses include unexpected loss or acquisition of a valued object or position as well as life-threatening disease or death.

Examples of ordinary and extraordinary stresses are listed in Table 3.

TABLE 3: TYPES OF STRESS ON COUPLE RELATIONSHIP

Object Stress

Ordinary	Extraordinary
Decision to purchase material goods jointly (clothing, food, furniture, house, investment, land, vehicle)	Sudden acquisition of valuable object
Decision to sell material goods jointly	Sudden loss of valuable object
Temporary "borrowing" of items with or without permission	
Use of joint funds	
Use or ownership of valued object	

Activity Stress

Ordinary	Extraordinary
Job demands: energy and time	Disease, disabling or prolonged
Living with extended family	Disparate lifestyles
Major goal achievement or failure	Financial irresponsibility
Move to another location	Legal problem: misdemeanor
Vacation decisions	Unemployment

Value, Role, and Extra-Couple Relationship Stress

Ordinary	Extraordinary
Change from one family life stage to another	Death of a child, friend, sibling
Change from one personal life stage to another	Disparate values
Child born or adopted	Financial loss, major
	Hospitalization or surgery
	Legal problem: felony

TABLE 3, *continued*

Ordinary	Extraordinary
Death of older family member	Severe illness in close family member
Disagreement concerning child-related problems (e.g., leaving home, school, social, etc.)	Sudden fame or wealth
Retirement	
Role change (e.g., wife goes to work)	

Unity Stress

Extraordinary

Alcohol or drug abuse
Disparate life goals
Infidelity
Institutionalization
Legal problem: jail sentence
Separation, prolonged (e.g., job relocation of one member of the couple)
Sexual dysfunction or deviation
Unwanted pregnancy

Type 1: Object Stress

This type of stress involves acquisition, use, ownership, or loss of some object valued by one or both partners. The problem concerns a thing. The crisis generated by Object Stress may be proportional not to the dollar cost of the object but to the personal value attached to it by one or both parties. Thus Jane's disposal of Harry's old baseball glove or bowling trophy may involve minor economic value but major ego involvement.

Object Stress particularly concerns biologic and economic needs, for example objects of food, clothing, shelter, or money. The most common sources of Object Stress in primitive societies involve food items, livestock, and "turf." In supposedly more civilized cultures, Object Stress usually concerns decisions about items of economic importance, items that are difficult or impossible to replace, or items that have high sentimental value.

Object Stress arises in couples at all level of interaction. Its threat to couple continuity is greatest at the more superficial levels of interaction (Convenience and Supportive) and less in deeper interaction levels (Nurturative and Unitive).

George and Frank: During the years together following Frank's divorce, George and Frank shared a home and evolved a comfortable lifestyle. The road to compatability was somewhat rocky at first. There were frequent visits by Frank's son and ex-wife, who loudly expressed disapproval of George. On balance, George's involvement in theater brought frequent meetings, rehearsals, or parties to the house, which annoyed Frank, who had little interest in acting or directing. Both suffered social isolation as neighbors on both sides complained about the "two queers" living next door, speculating as their their influence on the neighborhood children.

One by one George and Frank accommodated to these annoyances. Their time of assessment came when neighborhood antipathy brought a series of threatening telephone calls and anonymous complaints to the police describing disorderly parties and indecent behavior—of which the two men were quite innocent. As neighborhood harassment increased, George and Frank took stock of their relationship. Should they separate? Move away? Or stay and fight? Was their association worth the effort?

They concluded that it was, passing from the stage of assessment to recommitment. Their resolve strengthened, they confronted their neighbors, and invited them to attend the parties they had condemned; they began to take an interest in neighborhood activities. Before long, the anonymous calls and complaints ceased, and the George-Frank couple became accepted by the neighbors and by each other.

It was during this stable stage of recommitment that a major Object Stress arose. With relatively equal incomes, George and Frank had long pooled their finances into common savings and checking accounts. Household, clothing, and travel expenses were met as needed; neither of the two men was extravagant, and they incurring relatively equal monthly expenses. But then a new major expense arose: Frank's son graduated from high school and entered college. The prospect of a $3,000 yearly college tuition bill plus living expenses would sorely strain their modest budget. Frank recognized that George had no obligation to share the support of his son's college education. George saw the added financial burden as a threat to the relationship.

Type 2: Activity Stress

Activity Stresses concern planning, doing, moving, staying, and living. Achievement or failure may be involved. Ordinary causes of Activity Stress include conflicts concerning actions on the job, in social activities, or with friends or other family members. "Why must you spend so much time working?" "Can't your mother visit someone else this summer?"

Extraordinary Activity Stress may involve actions or failure to perform actions related to disease, finances, employment, or lifestyle. When Harry was out of work for two months one year, his couple relationship with Jane faced a crisis as Jane expressed her feelings: "If he doesn't go back to work soon, I'll go crazy." We find the "underfoot husband" an all-too-frequent Activity Stress of the recently retired couple.

Activity Stress is common in couples who interact on a supportive or nurturative level, particularly when the relationship is asexual and the needs met are largely economic and social. Thus Activity Stress is particularly likely to occur in the partnership couple whose reason for being is a financial, social, or educational venture and whose focus is on a single activity:

Roger and Gloria: The restaurant owner and waitress, whose long years together in a Nurturative Interaction had brought them to the stage of recommitment, faced a major Activity Stress which threatened their relationship. On his 57th birthday, Roger realized that retirement was only a few years away. An inquiry to the Social Security Administration revealed that he would qualify for a modest monthly payment at age 65, but he had little in the bank to bolster his income during the retirement years. With this in mind he resolved to increase his working hours, with the extra income earmarked for the retirement fund. Roger reasoned that his retirement nest egg, supplemented by Social Security payments, would allow a comfortable although not affluent retirement.

He announced to Gloria his plan to open the restaurant for Sunday brunch. His scheme called for an elaborate hot buffet with a hefty price tag. Roger explained, "Those few hours on Sunday morning can bring the best profit of the week."

Gloria objected. Sunday was her day to attend church, her major social activity outside of the restaurant. Furthermore, her strict Christian ethic prohibited working on Sunday. Her response was firm: "I won't work Sunday mornings and that's that!"

Type 3: Value, Role, and Extra-couple Relationship Stress

Stresses of this type are inevitable in all couple relationships. They often occur as a prelude to and during the couple life stage of assessment. Sheehy has described a number of these stresses as passages: the creative crisis, the spiritual crisis, the crossroads for women, the problems of generativity, and the courage for a career change.[18] The ordinary Type 3 stresses involve decision and differences concerning children, siblings, and parents, and role changes within the family structure. Less commonly encountered is extraordinary stress such as a major legal problem, sudden wealth or fame, devastating financial loss, or serious illness.

Role changes are a significant source of stress, often occurring when the mid-life crisis of a partner coincides with the Assessment Stage of couple life. At this time society allows and perhaps encourages subtle role shifts between men and women. The man who has fulfilled the traditional active role as breadwinner, protector, and high achiever may assume a more passive stance. The children are gone, financial pressures are lessened, and his status goals have been achieved or deemed beyond reach. At this time, the woman may be making her mid-life move from a mothering, nurturing, and an otherwise socially passive role to become a more active participant in the world about her. As the family passes from the launching to empty nest stage, the wife in the traditional household may celebrate her emancipation by returning to work, study, and social activities. In tune with the times, she may make more active sexual demands upon her husband as well as challenging his authority within the household. Such role shifts are a major source of Type 3 stress, as occurred in the case of Harry and Jane.

Harry and Jane: When Harry arrived home after work, he sensed something was afoot. Jane had prepared a before-dinner drink—an uncommon treat—and cooked a large steak dinner. "Look out," he thought, "she's setting me up for something big."

Over dinner she broke the news. "I've been offered a job! Harry, you remember my classmates, Larry and Sue. They married right after high school graduation and Larry now has an insurance office downtown. I was talking to Sue last week, and she said that Larry is looking for a secretary. She asked if I might be interested and offered me the job. The pay is super, and it's just the kind of work I know how to do. But, Harry the hours are not the best. I would be working five days a week and wouldn't be home until 4:30 each afternoon."

Harry replied, "I don't think I like the idea. If you come home at 4:30 each day and the children are home from school at 3:10, they'll have to go to a neighbor. We have always agreed that it's important that the children feel secure at home, and I don't think that the advantages of the job will offset what it will do to the children. Sure, we could use the money, but I don't think it's fair to the children."

"Well, Harry, what about me? While you have been working and meeting interesting people each day, I've been stuck here at home. It was bad enough before the children were both in school, but now there's just not much for me to do. After the breakfast dishes are washed and the beds are made, I putter around and try to keep busy until they come home in the afternoon. I need something to do to keep me in touch with the world, to keep me from becoming just a stale frumpy housewife. Harry, I want this job for *me*. And I feel strongly about it."

Harry and Jane faced a classic mid-life stress of married couples—the identity crises of one partner which precipitates a Type 3 Role Stress for the couple. Jane was at what Sheehy calls the "crossroads for women," often occurring at about age 35.[18] She and her husband were in different personal life stages and he might well suffer his mid-life identity crises five years or even a decade later. Nevertheless, a major couple stress arose and the couple had to cope.

Type 4: Unity Stress

Type 4 Unity Stress threatens the relationship itself and places the couple in greatest jeopardy. In Table 3 it is noteworthy there are no ordinary Unity Stresses, no expected assaults on the union itself. All such stresses are extraordinary and include such internal and external events as infidelity, separation, sexual dysfunction, institutionalization, or incompatable life goals. Stress of this type is likely to cause termination of couple unions at the Convenience and Supportive levels of interactions, particularly if it occurs during the vulnerable couple life stages of accommodation or assessment. In these instances, keeping the couple together calls for exceptionally effective methods of dealing with stress (often involving professional intervention) and bilateral firm family support.

Joseph and Maria: When Joseph agreed to move in with his daughter Maria, there was a tacit understanding that the arrangement was temporary. "Maria, I will only stay here until you find a husband. When that time comes, I'll go."

On that basis Maria and her father began their period of adjustment. He closed his eyes to her American ways, her occasional staying out late at night, and her failure to attend church on Sunday. Maria, for her part, learned to live with the odor of her father's cigars and his stack of dirty dishes in the sink.

Seven years later Maria's romance with a new boyfriend took a serious turn. They began seeing each other nightly and he called her at work during the lunch hour each day. Physical intimacy progressed to sexual union and Maria visited her physician for a birth control pill prescription. Within a few months Maria received a proposal of marriage and brought the news to her father.

Although Joseph and Maria had agreed, in their original contract, that he would step aside if a suitor emerged, there nevertheless evolved a distinct couple relationship which met needs and fears of loss, and that possessed an inertia that belied the original verbal agreement. Clearly, both Joseph and Maria suffered ambivalence concerning the marriage proposal and a severe couple stress existed.

STRESS AND THE COUPLE

The four types of stress cause disruption of smooth personal, family, and couple function. The greater the force of the stress, the stronger its impact. Since either ordinary or extraordinary stress represents a disruptive force, its value in the Couple Stability Index is a minus quantity, as follows:

Type of Stress	Couple Stability Index Value
Objects	-1
Activities	-2
Values, roles, and extra-couple relationships	-3
Couple Unity	-4

When considering the significance of a stress, we must think about the couple's value orientation.[8] The impact of a stress on the couple varies according to their cultural background and personal values. For one couple an unplanned pregnancy may be a joyous event while for another it may present a major crisis. Similarly, retirement may bring havoc to one household and not to another. Thus, a pregnancy or retirement—or sudden fame, job change, or even separation—may represent a greater or lesser stress in various couples, according to their value orientation, and these differences must be considered in any couple analysis or in counseling.

**COUPLE
FOCUS:
CHAPTER
SEVEN**

1. What are the common signs of stress?

2. What are the usual ways of coping with stress?

3. Which of these stress adaptation mechanisms have you used recently?

4. How does stress adaptation affect couple stability?

7

THE DOCTOR REMOVED HIS glasses and placed them on the desk. He looked directly at Jane and said, "I can find no physical cause for your headaches and I think they are related to what is going on in your life. There is tension between you and your husband and, in fact, between your personal ambitions and some feelings of guilt. When these conflicts are resolved, your headaches should disappear. Now, let's talk about how to deal with these problems. . . ."

All types of stress described in the previous chapter have their impact upon the individual, the family, and the couple. In response, the person, couple, or family tries to cope with stress and lessen its impact.

STRESS AND THE COUPLE

What Stress Causes

Stress reveals itself in many ways, many subtle and some obvious. The three general ways that stress is shown are physical, emotional, and behavioral.

PHYSICAL SIGNS OF STRESS. Stress of any type may cause physical illness. In a classic study of over 5,000 patients, Holmes and Rahe found that the onset of disease is likely to be correlated with a stressful life event such as the death of a spouse, divorce, marital separation, jail term, death of a close family member, or personal injury. These life events are all examples of extraordinary stresses threatening couple unity. The leading events—death of a spouse (or in the context of this book, the couple partner) and divorce or separation—not only threaten but destroy the couple unity. The other three life events—jail term, death of a close family member, or personal injury—place the couple relationship in jeopardy. Other stresses likely to precede physical illness, according to Holmes and Rahe, include marriage, being fired from a job, marital reconciliation, and retirement.[6]

EMOTIONAL SIGNS OF STRESS. Common emotional stress symptoms include anxiety and depression. For the individual, couple, and family, severe illness in a family member is a common cause of psychological problems. Emotional disorders develop in almost one-third of all individuals who have juvenile diabetes, and the parents of diabetic children have an increased risk of couple conflict and termination.[3, 11] In half the families of children with childhood cancer, at least one family member has required psychiatric treatment, according to a recent study.[1]

The individual experiencing major stress—failure of a business venture, a job offer in another state, or death of a close family friend—may suffer sleeplessness, loss of appetite, or tremulousness. As Maria contemplated her choice of marrying or remaining with her father, she lost weight, slept poorly, and sometimes cried for no apparent reason.

BEHAVIORAL SIGNS OF STRESS. Changes in how we behave often occur in times of stress. The individual preoccupied with a major economic or social decision may be withdrawn, quick-tempered, and neglectful of his couple partner. Role change stresses often lead to faultfinding and hostility. Profound and extraordinary stresses may cause major behavioral shifts, sometimes to cope with the stress itself and, in other instances, as apparent self-imposed penance to relieve guilt feelings. A study of families with children having cystic fibrosis revealed that 40 percent of parents in these families had severly curtailed couple social activities.[22] Gloria's behavior changed following Roger's proposal to serve Sunday brunch: She seemed to take less interest in her work—orders were confused, and food arrived at tables cold.

Coping with Stress

The person who touches a hot stove will quickly pull the hand away. The heat is a stress and withdrawal is the adaptation. If the room is too warm the thermostat may be adjusted to a lower level; this also is stress adaptation. Couples react to stress in various ways, and their adaptations may be guided by group interaction, professional counseling, or self-help.

GROUP EFFECT. The use of groups to deal with specific life stresses is increasing. One of the earliest of such organizations was Alcoholics Anonymous, which began in 1935 in Akron, Ohio. It is based on a concept of self-determination, an instinct for the benefits of group therapy, and overtones of religious fervor. Alcoholics Anonymous commands full commitment from its members, offers emotional support from others who have shared the agonies of alcoholism, and involves all family members willing to help. The beneficial effects of group interaction are attested to by the enviable record of Alcoholics Anonymous in dealing with the difficult problem of alcoholism, and their success far surpasses that of traditional medical therapists.

Groups available to help with other disease stresses that couples may face include Weight Watchers and other diet groups, mastectomy clubs, and diabetes associations. Psychosocial couple problems may be discussed in groups such as Parents Without Partners, Parents Anonymous, Marriage Encounter, and church affiliated couples' clubs.

PROFESSIONAL COUNSELING. Professional assistance can aid the couple during times of stress. The dual benefits of counseling and the group effect may be available through group therapy under professional guidance. Individual counseling of couples may be performed by marriage counselors, psychologists or psychiatrists, family physicians, or religious leaders. Professional assistance may be focused on one aspect of the couple relationship, such as with sex therapy or behavioral modification. Therapists should have an understanding of couple concepts, training in basic problem-solving and communication techniques, and the ability to relate to the couple as individuals and together.

SELF-HELP EFFORTS. A current focus of the medical profession is on patient education, affording maximum opportunity for individual self-help. Such emphasis is enhanced by general medical guides covering a wide variety of subjects.[19] Specific self-help therapy in dealing with individual and marital stresses has been discussed in recent books that offer coping methods which can be used alone or along with professional guidance.[9, 10, 17]

STRESS ADAPTATION METHODS

Every stress, major or minor, is met with some adaptive method. A person with a problem will try to cope. Often the adjustment is unconscious and/or habitual, such as drawing back the burned hand; in other instances major physical or emotional alterations are necessary to meet a crisis.

Not all stress adaptation is helpful and effective. In fact, many times stress is met with pathologic adaptation and the result is harmful. Sometimes the stress is denied altogether, and this, in itself, is a type of adaptation. The use of helpful mechanisms increases the likelihood that the stress will be met successfully and conquered.

Pathologic Adaptations

Six pathologic adaptations are commonly used by couples in time of stress—blame and punishment, combat, reaction formation, resignation, rigidification, and transference. All interfere with effective problem solving.

BLAME AND PUNISHMENT. In the family milieu this may take the form of scapegoating—choosing a person to assume the blame and punishment when things go wrong. Within a twosome, the individual meeting stress with blame and punishment has no choice but to denounce his couple partner. Blame and punishment is a common reaction to stress, and like other pathologic adaptations, is particularly seen in couples at Levels 1 and 2 (Convenience and Supportive) of couple interaction and during the Accommodation and Assessment Stages of the couple life cycle.

The drama of blame and punishment follows familiar scripts: A problem has occurred and some action might have changed the outcome. For example, if she had not been talking while he was driving, the automobile accident would not have occurred; thus the fault is hers. Or, if he had fixed the frayed electric cord, there would have been no fire.

With blame there is ample opportunity to act out roles and one partner may always assume the aggressor stance and the other, a passive role. Punishment may involve withdrawal of privileges, services, or love.

COMBAT. Fighting is a favorite couple sport. The initial encounter may consists of subtle jabs, progressing to an all-out frontal assault with words or even physical abuse. One partner may respond with combat in reaction to any other coping method while the other partner may continue his original adaptation, join in the combat, or shift to another method.

Coping by combat is uncommon in the early stages of a relationship. It is most likely to occur during the Accommodation or Assessment Stage of the couple life cycle.

Charles and Michael: The two boys faced a disparity of lifestyles, particularly regarding their respective dedication and aversion to loud rock music. As Charles' academic efforts increased, the music's duration and decibels rose. For his roommate, study meant quiet. Initially, Michael responded by studying at the library, returning at bedtime to encounter Charles' friends who came to keep him company while he studied.

Before long, the conflict erupted. The two boys argued frequently and loudly. The theme of their discussions never varied and each clung tenaciously to his viewpoint. After several weeks of verbal combat, no solution was in sight.

REACTION FORMATION. Reaction formation is the overt expression of ideas or actions that are the opposite of repressed true feelings. The individual adapting to stress with reaction formation can readily explain any major crisis—disease, disability, financial loss, or even death—as a blessing in disguise. Reaction formation is a way of coping with the death of a close family member or friend, allowing individuals to relieve anxiety by describing death as a release from suffering. We often encounter reaction formation at funerals, particularly of older persons. In couple conflicts, reaction formation may take the form of solicitous concern to mask anger.

RESIGNATION. Michael coped with the noise conflict with resignation, until he decided to speak out. Resignation is the ultimate passive or placating stress adaptation, and those who cope this way are frequently couple partners of persons who blame and punish, the respective aggressor and placator roles filling psychological needs for both. The person using resignation meets stress by admitting the futility of action and resolving to live with the problem. Deciding to "live with it" allows some conservation of emotional energy, but at the expense of accepting unhappy results which could have been avoided by better ways of coping.

RIGIDIFICATION. The assignment of each crisis to a category in some predetermined scheme is how some persons deal with adversity. Common rigidification structures include religion, philosophy, and politics. Thus life events may be described as the will of God, Allah, or Buddha. The acts of individuals may mark them as wither Facists or Communists. Individuals may be reduced to cultural stereotypes or their actions to psychological clichés. This adaptation mechanism allows a person to reduce emotional tension by placing the stress in a familiar pigeonhole.

Roger and Gloria: Roger and Gloria, the restaurant owner and waitress, were in an activity conflict concerning a change in working hours. Roger believed that his hope of a comfortable retirement hinged upon a successful Sunday brunch enterprise. Gloria balked. Roger implored, "Without help, I can't manage Sunday mornings alone." Clearly a couple stress existed.

Gloria explained her refusal on religious grounds. She quoted the scriptures to Roger, explaining that God intended the Sabbath as a day of rest and that to work on Sunday morning would be sinful. Roger's every suggestion was countered with an objection expressed with the conviction achieved only by those who know that God is on their side.

TRANSFERENCE. Transference is a shift of feelings from one person to another or sometimes to an object or idea. In couples, this means one partner shifts feelings that are directed at the other partner onto someone or something else, or transfers feelings toward an outside object onto the couple partner. Transference is an ideal way to express anger which otherwise might be directed toward the couple partner, but by transference is channeled elsewhere. When Jane received a speeding ticket, Harry's anger focused on the policeman who, as Harry said, "should be catching criminals instead of arresting innocent citizens."

Feelings may be transferred to objects or events as well as persons, and transference may allow one or both couple partners to ascribe a problem to an illness or accident, to children or a mother-in-law, to chance or fate.

George and Frank: The stress in this alliance concerned Frank's use of couple money to pay his son's college tuition. George objected, but rather than directing his anger toward the problem or even Frank, he focused his feelings on Frank's son. "That long-haired hippie son of yours has no business going to college. His high school marks were dreadful and his intellectual curiosity wouldn't fill a thimble. The boy has no respect for our generation and before he goes to college, he should do a lot of growing up." From time to time George's rhetoric would touch on the $3,000 annual tuition, but his most heated comments were directed toward the boy.

Failure to Admit a Problem

Also called denial, failure to recognize and confront a problem is a way many people cope—or do not cope—with stress. One or both parties simply deny that a problem exists. The person using denial as a stress adaptation mechanism probably has dealth with crises in this way throughout his life. Often choices have been made by default, with the person staying in situations—home, job, relationships—by simple failure to make decisions.

Roger and Gloria. Failure to make decisions plagued Roger's life. Over the years he might have expanded the restaurant, purchased new equipment, or otherwise improved the business, but opportunities were allowed to slide by. Thus, his relationship with Gloria had evolved not by intent but by default—his failure to confront the fact that Gloria was not only frequently tardy but inefficient and not altogether tidy. In fact, Roger's decision to change the working hours was a departure from his usual pattern, but he reverted promptly to his usual pattern by failing to confront the crisis formented by the proposed change.

When Gloria asserted, "God will punish us if we work on Sunday," an incredulous look crossed Roger's face.

Patiently and carefully he explained his proposal, emphasizing the increased income and security for them both. But Gloria remained adamant. Her refusal puzzled Roger as did her rigid reasoning, and he retreated in confusion.

Lucille and Martha: Lucille and her divorced daughter Martha faced stress early in their relationship, over values, roles, and relationships involved in rearing Martha's children. Autonomy was the major issue. As a modern mother, Martha believed that her youngsters, then aged 7, 10, and 12, should be allowed to watch television until 9 p.m. on weeknights, attend evening movies on weekends, and trade overnight visits with friends from time to time. Lucille objected, citing the dangers of these practices to her grandchildren's emotional and physical well-being.

Martha bristled when the children looked to their grandmother for decisions; Lucille was irked by Martha's frequent absence from the home. The stress on the relationship became apparent when Martha's 12-year-old daughter, Jenny, was invited for a weekend trip by a classmate and her family. Martha said "Go", and Lucille said "No."

Both women failed to recognize that a problem existed. Certainly they were aware of daily disagreements but neither coped with the problem—that their basic philosophies of childrearing reflected the customs of two different generations. Effective communication or problem solving techniques might have allowed them some insight. But instead both denied the presence of a problem as they continued day-to-day conflicts over the trivia of childrearing.

Recognition of the Problem

Problem recognition is the first step toward meeting stress effectively. The nature of the stress should be clearly identified and agreed upon by both parties. This may include naming the pathologic adaptations used by one or both partners, since such responses often add to the problem itself.

Problem recognition may include talking about unmet needs and goals which may be a source of anger for one partner or the other. With the problem defined, the couple may find that the tension is lessened or that a solution becomes apparent; or they may proceed to more active means of resolving conflict.

George and Frank: Frank's proposal to use their couple money to pay his son's college tuition bill was met by George's personal attack upon the son, a transference type of pathologic stress adaptation mechanism. Frank's insight into the problem was greater than that of George. Rather than responding in anger, Frank recognized the financial stress that using joint funds would place on the relationship. Moreover, he correctly identified George's personal attack as a transference of anger from the use of joint funds to the person of his son. And he wondered, "What can be done to smooth George's ruffled feathers yet meet my honorable obligations?"

Joseph and Maria: Both knew what the marriage would mean. When Maria decided to say yes, their time of living together was over. As a father, Joseph was pleased by the coming marriage of his daughter, but as an older man in a strange country, he felt some apprehension concerning the prospect of life alone.

Marie also felt torn, with joy at her long-awaited marital prospect and concern for her father's well-being. Both acknowledged that a problem existed. Discussion followed, initiated by Joseph, "Maria, it's not right for you to spend your life living with your father, and I think we should talk about your boyfriend and your future."

They agreed that the initial contract would be fulfilled and that their couple trajectory would end with the coming marriage.

Open Discussion

Each partner may use a different method of stress adaptation. Thus it is possible, as in the case of George and Frank, that one partner (Frank) recognizes the problem while the other (George) responds with a pathologic adaptation mechanism. Open discussions, as well as the problem solving and communication methods described below, require the cooperation of both partners.

Open discussion of a problem begins with identifying the stress, and citing unmet needs, the type of stress, and feelings that are present. Effective open discussion generally hinges on adherence to these five ground rules:

1. Bring disagreements into the open and confront them.
2. Stick to the topic.
3. Fight fairly. Do not inject past oratory, errors, or indiscretions.
4. Avoid personal invective.
5. Finish the discussion.

The discussion need follow no particular format, but open acceptance of each other's thoughts and opinions is vital to success.

John and Margaret: Their first month of married life brought a major couple stress. The impetus to buy a house came from Margaret, who had spent the years of her first marriage living in a three-room apartment while dreaming of being the mistress of her own elegant home.

With the encouragement of a helpful real estate salesman, she found her dream house: It had an entrance hallway, spiral staircase leading to four large bedrooms, a formal dining room, swimming pool, and acres of lawn. It was the house of her childhood fantasies.

John said, "No! I—that is, we—don't have that kind of money. We just can't afford the house."

Together they identified the problem. They discussed their budget as well as their housing needs, as they searched for a solution agreeable to both.

Problem Solving and Communication Techniques

Two of the most effective ways to cope with major stress are problem solving and communication techniques. Both involve methods which can be developed informally by trial and error or learned from books or teaching programs. Active participation of both partners is vital to the successful use of these techniques.

PROBLEM SOLVING. This is often a tool of marriage counselors and clinical psychologists. Writing is often used to supplement conversation. First the problem is identified. The next step is to describe goals. In some couples there will be general goal agreement—to buy a house she can be proud of and he can afford. For other couples the aims will be miles apart. When this occurs, the therapist will negotiate with the two partners to find ends toward which both are willing to work. In self-help problem solving, the couple must be willing to give and take until goals are shared in common.

The next step is to find correctable causes of stress. Each partner will compose a list independently, then share it with the other, and with the counselor if one is involved. In the childrearing conflict between Lucille and Martha, the grandmother's list of conflicts might include allowing children too much freedom, permitting children to talk back to their mother, and giving them too much spending money. Martha's list might contain excessive smothering of the children, too many unnecessary restrictions upon their behavior, and failure to treat them according to their ages. The lists of conflict causes for a couple living together in the period of adjustment—Charles and Michael—might tell of annoying habits, traits, and actions.

The next step can be either negotiation or acceptance. With negotiation, the two partners trade item for item on their lists. Lucille would try to stop smothering the children, if Martha would curtail their television viewing. Roommates or young marrieds may agree that one partner will stop throwing dirty socks under the bed while the other will replace the cap on the toothpaste after use.

The alternative problem solving step is acceptance: There is again a tradeoff, item for item. But in this instance the negotiated agreement is acceptance of behavioral foibles: He will tolerate stockings drying in the shower if she will accept beard clippings in the sink

Harry and Jane: Their couple stress involving Jane's identity crises was approached with this technique of problem solving. They had developed the technique in their marriage and had used it from time to time when problems arose. Whenever there seemed to be a conflict, one or the other would say, "Let's write about it." So effective had the method been, that they had taught it to their children and used it to solve occasional problems between parents and children.

Harry and Jane agreed that the stress was one of changing roles and that their common goal was fulfillment of Jane's changing psychosocial needs without neglecting parental obligations.

Jane's problem list began:

1. Bored being home all day.
2. Need interaction with people older than age 10.
3. Need to do something meaningful with my life.

Harry's problem list started:

1. Someone must meet and be with the children each day after school.
2. The housework must be done each day.
3. Jane needs something more to give her life meaning—and more zing.

Negotiation followed: Items 1 and 2 on Jane's list and the first item on Harry's list were negotiated by agreeing to hire an after school babysitter three days a week. This would allow Jane to accept a job on a part-time basis. The second item on Harry's list prompted his offer to help with the housework which, as he said, was the least he could do to compensate for the added income Jane's new part-time job would bring the family. Items 3 were in agreement.

Thus problem solving led to a negotiated compromise consistent with the goals of the couple.

COMMUNICATION TECHNIQUES. There are several methods by which couples express thoughts and feelings to one another. Writing is often involved. Communication techniques are often used in problem solving, but in addition, can help two individuals to know each other as totally as possible. A couple using communication techniques may engage in daily or weekly sessions, at which time they exchange feelings concerning their lives, their couple relationship, and one another.

Communication techniques may evolve as a couple progresses through the various levels of interaction and through the stages of couple life, and are most likely to be used by couples at the Unitive Level of Interaction and during the Assessment and Recommitment Stages of couple life.

The format of communication techniques will vary from one couple to another, but the basic aspect of telling and accepting feelings remains constant. Feelings—emotions concerning an act, object, person, or concept—are discussed as openly as possible, with each couple member trying to dig beneath the surface and reveal some small facet of his inner self. There must be a firm agreement that expressed feelings will be accepted without judgment; mutual trust is vital to exposing deeply personal emotions. One couple may express feelings orally. Another couple may write their feelings and then exchange notebooks or letters, the act of writing allowing each to describe feelings that might be difficult to express out loud. The technique—sometimes called dialogue—may be used to exchange feelings on a topic of mutual interest or a source of couple stress.

Phyllis and Nancy: Phyllis and Nancy, a teacher-student intergenerational homosexual couple, faced a major Unitive Stress—the prospect of separation. Nancy's graduation would, of necessity, separate the two women who had come to depend upon one another for emotional support.

The separation stress was recognized by both, and the coped by using communication techniques that they had developed during their years together. Each began writing in a notebook, sharing her thoughts, fantasies, and feelings, and focusing on their relationship and particularly the prospect of separation. When they met together on evenings and weekends, they exchanged and discussed the notebooks, exploring the deepese emotions expressed. Over the weeks prior to graduation, each woman confronted her personal feelings and their significance for the relationship.

ORGANIZATIONS THAT USE PROBLEM SOLVING AND COMMUNICATION TECHNIQUES

As society has come to recognize the stabilizing influence of communication techniques, several organizations have arisen which are devoted to improving intracouple relationships.

One such organization is the Marriage Encounter movement, which began in the United States in 1967 under the sponsorship of the Catholic Church and has enjoyed rapid growth so that at present approximately one million persons of various religious forths around the world have been "encountered." Entry into the Marriage Encounter movement begins with the Weekend—44 hours of intense communication under the tutelage of team couples and a religious advisor. Marriage Encounter teaches the dialogue technique, with communication on a chosen topic involving a 10-minute writing period and 10-minute oral discussion focusing on feelings. Following the weekend, encountered couples are encouraged to maintain involvement with the movement, including couple and family social functions, renewal programs, and presentations to prospective encounter couples.[4]

Another organization that helps couples communicate is ACME, the acronum of the Association of Couples for Marriage Enrichment, founded in 1973 by David and Vera Mace. While serving as Director of the American Association of Marriage and Family Counselors, David Mace noted an American tendency to marry young and make a mess of it, undergo a psychologically traumatic divorce, then seek and often eventually find happiness the second time around. Starting from an assembly of 10 couples at a mountain retreat, ACME developed as a loose federation of programs designed to strengthen marriage with improved communication methods.

A third organization is the Minnesota Couple Communication Program, developed by Sherod Miller, Elam Nunnally, and Daniel Wackman. From its origin as a program to prepare engaged couples for the demands of married life, the program has grown to a series of weekend sessions which train instructors. Graduates leave these sessions qualified to direct programs of four three-hour workshops supplemented by a basic sourcebook. The approach involves three steps: recognizing the need for self-awareness, encouraging self-expression, and receiving the message with appropriate feedback.

Other programs to enhance couple communication have been developed in many communities and universities. However, these programs have emphasized the traditional married heterosexual couple. Other couple relationships have been generally ignored and left to develop their own communication techniques, often quite successfully.

EFFECT ON COUPLE STABILITY

Stress adaptation may affect couple stability in a favorable or unfavorable way, as follows:

Stress Adaptation Method	Couple Stability Index Value
Pathologic adaptation by both partners	-2
Pathologic adaptation by one partner	-1
Denial	0
Recognition of the problem by one partner	+1
Problem recognition and open discussion by both partners	+2
Use of problem solving and communication techniques	+3

Because each couple partner may react differently to stress, the adaptation of each must be considered. The highest value is ascribed to couples using problem-solving and communication techniques, and a Couple Stability Value of +3 reflects the likelihood that couples using these methods will stay together. When both partners recognize and discuss the problem, the score is +2. A +1 is achieved if one partner recognizes the conflict (and is ready for open discussion), but this positive score may be offset if the mate uses a pathologic method.

Failure to confront a problem is scored as a zero. Denying the existence of a stress or crisis will not necessarily aggravate the problem, though denial does not deal effectively with the delinquent child, alcoholic wife, or jailed husband. The failure of Lucille and Martha to deal with their differences earns for them a zero score.

Pathologic adaptations by one or both partners are ascribed negative scores, since such unhealthy adjustments only intensify problems between the couple. Charles and Michael, who both meet stress with combat, receive a -2 value. For Roger and Gloria, his denial (0 value) and her pathologic rigid reaction to stress (-1 value) earn them a -1 net score.

The Harry-Jane and Phyllis-Nancy couples each receive a +3 stress adaptation score because of their use of problem solving and communication techniques. Joseph and Maria both recognized the dilemma posed by the suitor's proposal and discussion followed, allowing them a +2 value. John and Margaret also earned a +2 value as they resolved the stress involved in buying a house by confronting the problem. Frank's recognition of the stress in his relationship gains him a +1 score, but this is offset by George's pathologic reaction (-1), giving them a value of zero.

Even the highest stress adaptation score of +3 fails to offset the -4 value of Unity Stress. Factors other than adaptive mechanisms influence the response to stress, and notable among these is the couple support provided by the family.

COUPLE FOCUS: CHAPTER EIGHT

1. What is a family?

2. What is an "effective family"?

3. What is the influence of family on the couple?

4. What are the support systems that can bolster the couple relationship?

8

JANE'S MOTHER INITIATED a heart-to-heart talk with her daughter. "I think I know what you're going through," she said. "There was a time—it seems so long ago—when keeping house and caring for your father and the family just didn't seem to be enough. I wondered if my life was serving any purpose. But your father and I talked about how I felt. And somehow the feelings passed and my life began to seem more meaningful.

"Now you are facing the same sort of personal crisis, and you will have to work it through yourself—and with Harry. But keep in mind that you have a wonderful husband who cares about you, and two lovely children. Don't do anything that will hurt that part of your life. Remember that Harry and the children are family, and family comes first."

FAMILY AND ITS ROLE

Family support—or lack of support—can make the difference between separating and staying together. Each partner in the couple is part of a family prior to entering into the couple union, and these ties remain. The family system may be different for each partner, as with Jane and Harry, or may be identical, as in couples involving siblings or parent and child.

Also, a family may spring from the couple itself as the union produces children.

Whatever their origin, relationship, and proximity, the family of each partner in a couple relationship helps determine the stability of couple life.

The Concept of Family

The most useful definition of family is "a significant group of intimates with a history and a future."[16] Building upon this definition, Carmichael has identified four characteristics of family—affinity, intimacy, reciprocity, and continuity—which allow us to determine the persons who fulfill a family role for each couple partner.

AFFINITY. This element of family refers to closeness. To be termed a family, individuals must be identifiable as a group of two or more. The traditional family begins as a man and woman agree to live together. However, social changes have brought new types of families just as they have fostered a variety of couple relationships. Thus a group of single individuals living together in a room, apartment, or commune fulfills this characteristic of family.

INTIMACY. This second element of family life involves some degree of interaction beyond simply sharing of food and shelter. There is a sense of concern, and an involvement in the trials and triumphs of others in the group.

McGinnis has described family intimacy as being open or closed.[14] Similar concepts have been identified by Minuchin, who discusses internal and external boundaries.[15] The closed family with impermeable internal and external boundaries is characterized by closed doors, defensive alliances, and a policy of minding one's own business; a specious sense of family closeness is generated by excluding outside influences.

The open family with permeable boundaries has open doors, a high degree of give and take, and involvement of family members in one another's business; the family is attuned to and readily influenced by social and cultural changes.

Each family we know has both some open and some closed characteristics, certain permeable and impermeable boundaries. In a family faced with school failure by an adolescent child, the excessively closed family with impermeable external boundaries may join forces, finding excuses for the child's school failure and blaming the teachers and administration. In the same situation, the family with excessive openness to the environment and permeable external boundaries may allow teacher opinion to undermine their emotional support of the child. Excessively closed living may lead to family fragmentation over minor issues such as meal schedules, dating behavior, or vacation plans. Excessive family openness with all–too– permeable internal boundaries fosters a lack of privacy and can stifle development of autonomy.

RECIPROCITY. Within any family there is a sense of interdependence, with acknowledgement of mutual needs. Needs filled by the family parallel those filled by the couple relationship—biologic, economic, sociologic, and psychologic— and each family member meets needs and has needs met in some fashion for and by each other family member.

CONTINUITY. Future is part of the definition of family and, as with the couple, both formal and implied contracts help determine continuity. For three secretaries sharing an apartment, the formal contract involves the apartment lease and the implied contract is an agreement that their "family" relationship will persist until one or more leaves because of job change, marriage, or some other reason. Following the departure of one individual, the remaining family members may recruit another person into the remaining family members may recruit another person into the relationship; or the family may end as the contract is dissolved.

The contracts for the usual parenting family involve a formal marriage license and the informal collection of historial, ethical, and moral building blocks that make up the foundation of marriage. The contract is fulfilled by meeting one another's personal needs; by bearing, raising, and launching children and by providing mutual support during the post-parental years.

The family trajectory—like the couple trajectory—may be completed or uncompleted. A completed family trajectory is fulfilled as four individuals share a dwelling for the duration of a one-year lease, then amicably go their separate ways (see page 199). The parenting family contract is fulfilled as the couple progresses through the eight stages of family life described in Chapter Five (see page 199). The uncompleted family is found when the faimly contract is unfulfilled because of illegitimacy, annulment, separation, divorce, or early death.

Filling the Family Role

Couple stability is influenced by whoever acts as family for each partner. Thus support of a couple relationship might come from co—workers, teammates, or roommates who fulfill the four above—mentioned elements of family, particularly when one's biologic family is distant or uninvolved. However, for most individuals, the extra—couple support system is the traditional family—children, siblings, parents, and even grand-children and grandparents—who influence couple relationships, whether they share the same roof or living far apart.

Each of us is born of parents and these ties will be of longer duration and greater intensity than peer relationships based on proximity and common interests. The traditional family teaches the earliest concepts of right and wrong and, when conflict arises, these early values become important. Peer values influence the couple but peers will supplant the traditional family as a support system only when a peer group with a history and future meets the characteristics of family for the couple partners.

Influence

How the family helps keep couples together depends on what happens in each of the four areas described by Carmichael.

AFFINITY. The family with close interpersonal bonds will usually have a greater influence on the couple than a family that is separated by geographical and emotional distance. However, the outcome may be unexpected. A large extended family living together in an open system may have a strong sense of family unity—but at the expense of couple involvement. One or both members of the couple may owe their primary allegiance to the family, and their couple interaction may be at the surface level.

On the other hand, affinity of family members may promote couple stability, particularly when the relationship is threatened by the Type 4 stress of illness, institutionalization, infidelity, or separation. When this happens, the potent stabilizing force of the large close family can tip the scales in favor of couple continuation.

INTIMACY. The closeness of Jane's mother and father develop a trusting, open relationship with Harry. The individual raised in an open family with a high degree of intimacy will be more likely to develop a Nurturative or Unitive couple relationship than the person raised in a closed family with rigid internal boundaries. Yet once a couple relationship is established, a continuing high degree of intimacy between one partner and his or her family may compromise the couple relationship. Thus the mother-in-law continues to cook and clean for her married son maintain with him an intimate, and indeed nurturative, couple relationship, one that threatens the son's couple relationship with his new wife.

RECIPROCITY. Teaching values to the child is the prerogative and the obligation of the parenting family. The child's response is the joy or woe of parents. The exchange of societal values between family and couple usually has a stabilizing effect, with communication of taboos against financial irresponsibility, sexual deviation, infidelity, and divorce. More than once children have said to their parents, "You taught us the importance of family, and now you are talking about divorce. We don't understand and can never approve, and we think you should start practicing what you have always preached."

CONTINUITY. The family with a long history of stable marriages is likely to rear offspring highly motivated toward couple continuity; such families are also likely to approve of couple relationships they believe are "proper"—particularly Category I couples. In this instance family values would decree that divorce is unthinkable unless overwhelming conflict occurred. Conversely, the family with aa highly stable couple history may disapprove of alternative couple relationships such as George and Frank (Category V) or even Joseph and his daughter Maria (Category IV). Families with a history of poor couple relationships are often indifferent to couple interactions and stress and may offer scant support; when this happens, the family role may be assumed by another group.

FAMILY SUPPORT SYSTEMS

The group fulfilling the role of family for an individual is called his "effective family." For each partner in the couple, the effective family may express approval or disapproval or may be ignorant, indifferent, or ineffective concerning the person's couple relationship.

Approval

A basic human motivation is parental approval of activities, and choice of a mate is high on the list of decisions for which we all seek parental sanction. Thus the words or deeds of parents or other effective family have a profound effect on couple continuity.

> *Roger and Gloria:* The conflict between Roger and Gloria concerning working hours strained their relationship. For both, biological families consisted of distant relatives in distant states. Roger's effective family was his long-standing clientele, while Gloria's effective family included both customers and her fellow church members. From both groups, there was unanimous approval of the relationship, which lent stability during their time of stress.
>
> *Phyllis and Nancy:* Phyllis and Nancy's teacher-student homosexual relationship evoked strong disapproval by Nancy's family, who were unable to comprehend what they described as their daughter's "unnatural urges." They sought counseling with their physician and their religious advisor and made a genuine effort to understand the relationship, but they could never approve. Phyllis' effective family were her fellow teachers and

students, whose attitude toward homosexuality was liberal and permissive. Although the exact nature of the relationship was merely suspected on campus, there was general approval of the presumed liaison.

Harry and Jane: Harry and Jane, offspring of work-oriented, churchgoing families, had courted and married with the enthusiastic approval of both families. The in-laws had become a quartet—as they met for holiday dinners, birthdays, and anniversaries of Harry, Jane, and their two children. When trouble threatened, the close-knit family group rallied for support.

Indifference, Ignorance, Ineffectiveness

In all too many instances, there is no effective family contribution to the couple relationship. This occurs particularly with the couple who live apart from their extended families, move often, and develop only surface relationships with friends at each new location. For these couples, the family may be unaware of couple stress or may be ambivalent about the outcome of a physically or emotionally distant individual's problems. Also, with frequent moves, the couple partners may have established no effective family among peers or co-workers. Thus family support—either approving or disapproving—may be lacking.

Sometimes when couple stress is present, family ambivalence may prevent helpful intervention. Parents whose daughter is separating from her husband may admit the benefits of her leaving a man they see as a heavy drinker, gambler, or fool, yet condemn the idea of divorce, particularly when children are involved. When such a dilemma is presented, the effective family—whether parents or peers—may be rendered ineffectual by value conflicts, and may appear indifferent or avoid the issue.

John and Margaret: When John married Margaret, his two children spoke out strongly, "She's so young that she could be our sister. Don't you think you should marry someone your own age?" Margaret's motives were suspect and the family refused to attend the wedding.

For Margaret, there was no such input. She had little contact with her parents after marrying her first husband. The divorce broke all ties, as her father spoke of the dishonor she had brought to her family. At the beginning of her couple relationship with John, her effective family consisted of a few close friends. This group shared John's family's suspicions of Margaret's motives, and their opinion was that a younger man would have been a more appropriate mate. Yet they cheered Margaret's happiness following the marriage, and thus her effective family was ambivalent.

Lucille and Martha: Martha's family was her three children, who were delighted with their life at Grandma's home. Lucille's family support came from her sister and brother, both married and living in other parts of town. Involved in their own lives and couple relationships, these two siblings expressed little interest in Lucille and her living arrangements.

Disapproval

Family failure to support a couple relationship is often based on a conflict of values, with failure of reciprocity between the couple partner and his family. The person who marries an individual of another race, engages in a homosexual relationships, lives unmarried with a sexual partner, or marries a person from another generation risks family disapproval based on differing values. Family disapproval may be based on fear that their member in the couple relationship will be demoralized, victimized, or alienated. There may be a belief that he or she is marrying above or below his or her own social class. Disapproval may be directed toward the individual's couple partner or toward the nature of the relationship, and may be expressed subtly or openly.

> *Charles and Michael:* College roommates Charles and Michael both derived family support from parents. The roommate relationship had the parental approval of Charles' parents, who believed that Michael would be a good influence on their son. His mother and father hoped that rooming with a serious student would improve Charles' sense of responsibility, his study habits, and ultimately his success in school.
>
> When Michael's family learned of the boys' disagreement, there was disapproval of Charles and of the roommate relationship. Michael's parents urged him to request a change of room, specifying that the new roommate should share his studious inclinations.
>
> *Joseph and Maria:* Joseph and Maria shared the same large extended family, and the opinion of this group was firm: Maria should not become trapped as housekeeper for her father, but rather should accept the offer of marriage and begin her own family. Joseph was invited to share a large home with other members of the family. Thus the distinction was drawn that while the family loved both Joseph and Maria, they believed their couple relationship should end.

George and Frank: George and Frank's relationship faced stern disapproval by the families of both men. From George's two older brothers came vocal disapproval of the homosexual relationship, based on a moral conflict. Frank's ex-wife and son, long resigned to his homosexuality, feared that his relationship with George might cause loss of funds for education. Although both families objected to their alliance, George and Frank stayed together.

EFFECT ON COUPLE STABILITY

Family approval or disapproval affects couple stability favorably or adversely. Thus a relationship such as that of Jane and Harry or Roger and Gloria, which enjoys two-sided family approval, receives support in times of stress, and the family may offer encouragement and lend physical aid in an effort to stabilize the relationship if crisis threatens.

Family support systems have the following impacts on Couple Stability Index Values:

Support	Couple Stability Index Value
Approval both families	+2
Approval one family	+1
Indifference/Ignorance/ Ineffectiveness	0
Disapproval one family	-1
Disapproval both families	-2

Since a +1 value is ascribed for each family offering favorable support, Harry and Jane, with approval of both families, have a +2 couple stability index value. In any couple, the effective family of one or both partners may be uninformed, ambivalent, or ineffectual, and a 0 value is scored for that person. Family disapproval for one partner is scored as -1 and for families of both partners as -2. Thus John's family's disapproval (-1) and Margaret's family's ambivalence (0) gives a couple stability value of -1. For Lucille an indifferent family score of 0 is added to Martha's family approval of +1. George and Frank, with bilateral family disapproval of their alliance, received a couple stability value of -2.

COUPLE FOCUS: CHAPTER NINE

1. How is the stability of a couple estimated?

2. How can recognition of couple dynamics aid in professional or self-help counseling?

3. What is society's stake in keeping couples together?

4. How can analysis of couple stability help preserve the couples in our lives?

CHAPTER NINE: KEEPING COUPLES TOGETHER

9

CAN COUPLE BONDS BE strengthened? Can weaknesses in a couple relationship be discovered—and reinforced—before problems occur? How can the analysis offered in this book help people improve and continue their couple relationships? A summary of the previous eight chapters will help answer these questions.

During his or her life each individual will form a series of couple relationships, existing simultaneously with different partners. Each relationship can be labeled according to one of eight couple categories, depending upon whether the relationship involves a partner of the same or opposite sex, a partner of the same or different generation, and an interaction that is sexual or asexual. The couple relationship begins to fill biologic, economic, and psychosocial needs. Once the couple duo forms, it becomes a self-sustaining entity that is likely to endure for its planned duration unless acted upon by significant stress. Whether or not stress will disrupt the couple union can be estimated by analysis of couple stability, based on (1) the level of interaction, (2) stage of the couple life cycle, (3) the type of stress, (4) the adaptation to stress, and (5) family support. Couple stability is independent of couple category and the Couple Stability Index Value is valid for the

Category I conventional married parenting couple as well as for the other kinds of couples described in this book.

Continuation of the couple relationship following Type 3 and particularly Type 4 stress is likely to be followed by progression of the couple from the Assessment Stage to the Recommitment Stage of the couple life cycle, with a correspondingly greater couple stability. In addition, triumph over severe stress will often result in couple interaction progressing to deeper levels such as from Level 2 Supportive to Level 3 Nurturative or from Level 3 Nurturative to Level 4 Unitive Interaction.

On the other hand, termination of the couple relationship may be followed by a different couple relationship between the same two persons, or separation of the two individuals who each then goes on to form couple relationships with other persons. For example, a married couple who divorce will continue a post-divorce association which may be amicable or hostile, and may, in fact, exist on any of the four interaction levels. And, following their divorce these two individuals are likely to form subsequent new couple relationships which may be in any of the eight categories.

COUPLE STABILITY VALUES

For each couple, a high positive Couple Stability Index Value indicates a greater likelihood of couple continuation; a Couple Stability Index Value at or near 0 indicates a risk of couple dissolution, while negative values suggest that current stress is likely to break couple bonds.

For each of the eight couples examined, one or possibly two of the five aspects of couple dynamics has been most instrumental in their couple stability. In other words, for each couple one aspect of the relationship has been their strongest asset or greatest threat.

Interaction Level

The more superficial interaction levels Convenience and Supportive are more easily disrupted than the deeper levels Nurturative and Unitive. The traditional marital relationship overtly aspires to the deeper levels of interaction, and frequently succeeds, and Category 1 couples tend to be prevalent and enduring.

Harry and Jane: For Harry and Jane their greatest asset was their Level 4 Unitive Interaction. Through conscious effort, they developed an openness to one another. There was the strength of couple interaction which comes only with open communication.

Thus Jane's role crisis, one of the predictable problems of mid-life, was met with communication and problem solving techniques. Jane described her feelings of social isolation and lack of personal productivity. She verbalized her realization that the years were speeding by and that life must offer more than living for her children. Harry accepted these feelings as open expressions of emotion, freely offered. He expressed his concern for the children's welfare, and described the anxiety that Jane's new assertiveness caused in him. Was his role as breadwinner being threatened? Might her aggressive posture be translated into other areas of their relationship? Their common goals were identified. There was give and take, and the problem was resolved as Jane agreed to modify her plans and accept a part-time rather than full-time job while Harry agreed to lighten some of her household burdens to compensate for the new duties she would assume. They agreed that after-school sessions with a babysitter three days a week would cause the children no great psychologic damage, and could indeed be beneficial if this allowed greater self-fulfillment for their mother.

Harry and Jane's Couple Stability Index Value is calculated on Table 4. Their total value of +7 indicates a high likelihood of couple continuation. The greatest numerical value—either positive or negative—is their inter-action level.

Consider the Couple Stability Index Value for the same couple during the early stages of dating. Their implied contract would be to spend pleasant days and evenings together from time to time and would not preclude couple relationships with other individuals. They would be beginning to discover one another's foibles. There would be no major approval or disapproval of families, who would see them aas "just dating." Add to this the stress of separation as Harry leaves for a two-year tour of duty in the Navy, a problem recognized and discussed by them both. In this hypothetical situation, they would have a Couple Stability Index Value of +2 (see Table 4) with a modest probability that the dating relationship would continue, probably with weekend and vacation meetings supplemented by cor-respondence.

The theoretical couple stability of Harry and Jane during dating includes hesitation of both families to become involved in the relationship. As we have noted, family approval or disapproval can have a telling influence on couple stability when the relationship is precarious. Thus in the above example, strong approval by both families would increase the Couple Stability Index Value to +4, with a relatively high likelihood of couple continuation. Bilateral family disapproval would decrease the value to 0, and couple continuation would become questionable.

Phyllis and Nancy: The relationship between Phyllis and Nancy faced a Type 4 stress to couple unity: separation. As illustrated in Table 10, they had a Level 4 Unitive Interaction and they met the stress with effective adaptation techniques. The Couple Stability Index Value of +4 indicates a good likelihood that their relationship would persist more or less in its same for, unless a change occurred in one or more of the relationship's facets.

If their early relationship had focused on its sexual aspects (with interaction on an activity level) and if both had faced the separation stress with pathologic adaptations such as blame and punishment of one another, then the Couple Stability Index would drop to -3 (as shown in Table 10) indicating that the two women would probably go their separate ways.

Couple Life Cycle

The stages of the couple life cycle influence couple stability, and a shift from one stage to another can have profound effects. Early in the relationship there is a strong commitment fo fulfill the implied and expressed couple contracts. During the subsequent phases of accommodation and assessment, there is a progressive risk of couple termination. Couples who survive these three phases and reach the phase of recommitment are likely to stay together.

Lucille and Martha: The couple stress of childrearing roles and values began soon after Martha and the children moved in. Martha was busy with the demands of her job and Lucille was beguiled by the excitement of her active grandparenting (and often parenting) role. Both failed to recognize the presence of stress, and this denial neither aggravated the conflict nor brought them closer to resolution. Continuation of the relationship with a Couple Stability Index Value of +3 was largely due to their phase in the couple life cycle, Commitment (see Table 11). A commitment had been made between the two individuals, and jointly with the children/grandchildren. Only major changes in couple dynamics would jeopardize the relationship. If the same value and role stress had occurred later, during the Assessment Stage of their couple life cycle, the Couple Stability Index Value would have been merely +1. In addition, if the children's opinion of life with grandmother had shifted from approval to rejection, (from +1 to -1), then the Couple Stability Index Value would drop to -1, indicating that Martha and her three children would probably look for another home.

George and Frank: The story of George and Frank (as summarized in Table 8) indicates a strong likelihood of couple continuation in spite of double-barreled family disapproval. The high value is largely due to their being in the Recommitment Stage of couple life, and also to their Nurturative Interactions. The stress they faced—Frank using couple money to pay his son's college tuition—posed but a minor threat to a powerful couple relationship. George eventually ceased transferring anger to Frank's son, and the rift between the two individuals closed. Frank recognized the problem, which included both the relationship stress caused by the object (financial) demands and George's pathologic adaptation to the stress. He proposed—and George reluctantly agreed—that a separate bank account be opened in George's name; each tuition check for Frank's son would be balanced by an equal amount deposited to George's personal account. Thus there would still be equal sharing of couple funds.

Type of Stress

Identification of stress type is essential in analysis of couple stability, since stress of modest force can threaten the weak relationship, while strong couple bonds will usually withstand the most potent types of stress.

John and Margaret: The intergenerational marriage of John and Margaret met an early stress. Selecting a house to fill the needs of both brought conflict. The two veterans of prior marriages had learned the futility of pathologic adaptation methods and of denial. The problem was quickly recognized and open discussion followed. As Margaret became aware that John's financial commitments to his business and his divorced family forced limitations on major purchases, and as John became aware of the psychologic and social implications of home ownership for his new wife, there evolved a profile of thee mutually acceptable house. A basic concept of size and cost was agreed upon and the couple began a search for their new home.

Their reaction to this stress at this time in their couple relationship is outlined in Table 6, with a Couple Stability Index Value of +5 indicating a strong likelihood that John and Margaret would stay together through their time of stress.

Their couple story showed minor stress occurring at the early Commitment Stage of marriage. If the couple relationship is projected forward in time through the accommodation phase of the years when—inevitably—John and Margaret are evaluating their union, a different picture may be seen. If during the Assessment Stage of couple life John and Margaret are faced with a Type 4 stress upon couple unity, such as John's severe heart attack which caused his hospitalization for six weeks followed by prolonged unemployment and prohibited sexual activity, the outcome might be different (see Table 6). Even with open discussion (stress adaption +2), there is a Couple Stability Index Value of zero, indicating an uncertain future. If one or both partners reacted to the stress of hospitalization and disability with a pathologic adaptation such as blame and punishment, the Couple Stability Index Value would be -3 or -4 with a probability that couple termination would confirm the dire forecasts of their family members and friends.

Joseph and Maria: As shown by Couple Stability Value of -1 (see Table 7), Joseph and Maria's living together was likely to end. Maria said, "Yes!" to the marriage proposal and Joseph began packing. The parent-child bond continued, however, and Joseph and Maria entered into a new father-daughter couple relationship, at the same time that Maria entered a new couple relationship with her bridegroom.

Stress Adaptation

In meeting stress the Couple Stability Index Values account for each partner's individual adaptation, and it is possible that one partner will recognize the problem (+1) while the other reacts pathologically (-1), yielding a zero value. A healthful approach by both partners will afford a +2 or even +3 value while pathological mechanisms utilized by both will be ascribed a -2 index value.

Charles and Michael: Their couple relationship faced an activity stress involving study and music, and they had a -1 Couple Stability Index Value (see Table 9). Both boys met stress with combat. Frequent arguments progressed to episodes of sullen silence punctuated by angry outbursts. Petty overt actts of anger followed, including refusing to accept one another's telephone messages and slamming doors. The deteriorating relationship threatened to lower the grades of both boys, as the anxiety of chronic stress became apparent. Resolution of the problem came when Michael formally requested a change of room. The Dean of Housing called Charles, who gratefully gave his okay for a change. New roommates were chosen for both boys who separated to begin couple relationships with other individuals.

The roommate relationship might have been saved by helpful stress adaptation. Intervention by a skilled counselor might have led both boys to examine the nature of their stress reaction, identify problems and goals, and possibly negotiate an amicable solution. Time might have been designated for study and for music respectively, with resolution of the conflict. The Couple Stability Index Value afforded by problem solving would be +4 (see Table 9); all that is changed is the way they cope with stress.

Family Support

Family support, while not as influential as the interaction level or phase of couple life, nevertheless affords a stabilizing, or sometimes disruptive, influence on a couple.

Roger and Gloria: When Roger and Gloria faced the stress of changed working hours, the effective families of both individuals properly avoided taking sides in the dispute, but rather demonstrated their bilateral support of the couple relationship.

Roger's effective family consisted of his customers, many of whom had eaten one or more daily meals in his restaurant for as long as two decades. From then came strong support of Roger and Gloria as an owner-waitress couple and this support was crucial in the final resolution of the problem.

Gloria's effective family—these same customers as well as her fellow church members—also supported the owner-waitress relationship.

Resolution of the problem came this way: a few long-term customers volunteered their services on Sunday mornings while Gloria attended church services. In return, Roger agreed to supply free breakfast for these workers, who would more than earn their meal. Furthermore, they persuaded Roger to close early one evening each week, convincing him that both he and Gloria would benefit from added time off in view of their expanded Sunday schedule. It was decided that the free evening would be Wednesday, which delighted Gloria since this allowed her to attend Wednesday evening choir rehearsal, an activity previously precluded by her work schedule. This unexpected benefit was interpreted as God's will, and a sign indicating divine approval of her helping out at brunch following Sunday morning services. The Couple Stability Index Value is shown in Table 5.

Support by the effective family aided in resolution of the problem. Theoretical family disapproval would have dropped the Couple Stability Value to +2. Thus even with family disapproval, this strong couple who had achieved the Recommitment Stage would probably have survived an activity stress regardless of stress adaptation or family support.

PROBABILITY OF CONTINUATION

Of the eight couples presented in this book, six have positive Couple Stability Index Values and fair to excellent likelihood of surviving the present stress. The highest value of +7 is attained by Harry and Jane, whose union exemplified the prevailing values of middle-class life. A high value of +5 is also attained by John and Margaret, whose marriage admittedly fulfills less ethereal needs than that of Harry and Jane. The Roger-Gloria couple relationship achieved a +6 value, demonstrating that an enduring and compatible relationship need not be sexual in nature. Impressive values of +4 were scored by both homosexual couples, George and Frank as well as Phyllis and Nancy; for George and Frank the good score is attributed to their couple life stage and interaction level, while Phyllis and Nancy achieved a high interaction level with effective stress adaptation mechanisms. The relatively new union of Lucille and Martha survived a major stress due to favorable family support and the impetus of the "honeymoon" stage; as this couple progresses through its life cycle, it is important that they develop effective mechanisms for coping with stress.

Charles and Michael, the roommate couple, separated, as predicted by a value of -1. These young men lacked involvement in the couple relationship and effective stress adaptation mechanisms; the result was unplanned termination of the couple union following modest stress. Also terminated was the Joseph-Maria couple relationship, as this union faced a major stress. However, the parting was by mutual agreement, their couple trajectory complete.

APPLICATION OF COUPLE DYNAMICS

Recognition of the five aspects of couple dynamics can aid in professional or self-help counseling. The Couple Stability Index not only tells the relative probability of continuation or termination of a relationship, but can pinpoint areas of weakness which can be strengthened. This type of analysis and intervention involves five stages:

(1) Recognition of Couple-Related Problem

The first stage of analysis and intervention is recognition by both partners that a problem exists, no easy task if one or both deny the existence of stress or the fact that individual stress adaptation mechanisms are being brought into play. The couple is a separate entity, albeit composed of two individuals, and it has an identity and life cycle and trajectory of its own. Thus stress may elicit individual symptoms of anxiety, depression, or irritability in one or both partners while couple stress may be manifested as hostility, aggression, indifference, or lack of communication between the two individuals. Recognizing these signs of stress helps signal when a problem exists. Counselors are often faced with the dilemma of one partner seeking help while the other denies the existence of the problem or refuses to join in problem solving. Such a plight poses a major challenge to the therapist: If he embarks upon single partner counseling, he becomes the ally of that individual in an aggressive or defensive alliance, and his effectiveness in counseling the partner is compromised. Yet, if he dismisses the symptom-suffering partner until the other enters therapy, a chance to help the couple may be lost. For the therapist resolution of this problem lies in joint efforts with the symptomatic patient to make the couple partner aware of the stress, his adaptations, and their impact upon the relationship.

(2) Assessment of the Relationship

The next step in analyzing a couple relationship is to assess its couple category, level of couple interaction, and stage of couple life cycle. Although couple category has no weight in the Couple Stability Index, it is useful in identification of the type of relationship, with implications for the couples value orientation. Significant couple values can include the taboos against homosexuality and incest; the general suspicion and disapproval of intergenerational marriages; the societal acceptance, albeit reluctantly, of nonmarried sexual partners living together; the tradition of convenience, same-sex roommate arrangements; and the favored tradition of the heterosexual, parenting married couple.

Identification of the interaction level is extremely helpful, since this is a major determinant of the Couple Stability Index Value. In counseling, we find that this level can be assessed at the end of the second session, as the therapist observes the two individuals' body language and eye contact, as well as their more overt interactions. For the couple undertaking self-help analysis, there must be an objective evaluation of their interaction level. From a practical standpoint, the couple undertaking self-analysis of their relationship, is indeed aspiring to a Unitive Interaction.

Assessment of the phase in the couple life cycle can be made readily during therapy or during self-help analysis. The Commitment Stage can usually be identified by knowing the duration of the relationship; and this stage is soon followed by the Accommodation Stage when the rosy glow is lost. The Recommitment Stage is usually achieved following successful weathering of major stress. In practice, most couples undergoing professional or self-help solution-directed couple analysis are—by definition—in the Assessment Stage of their relationship.

(3) Identification of Types of Stress

Stress identification helps reveal the threat to the relationship. In both professional therapy and self-help evaluation, the apparent type of stress may be a masquerade for deeper conflict. The couple may discuss between themselves or with a counselor such problems as energy and job demands or conflicts concerning living with an extended family member; yet these activity stresses may be the masks that hide deeper problems such as sexual dysfunction, infidelity, or disparate life goals. Early in assessment, the counselor or couple must recognize masquerades and identify the true sources of conflict.

(4) Enhancing Stress Adaptation Mechanisms

Change begins as the couple learns new and better ways to handle stress. The first step is to avoid pathological adaptation mechanisms and denial. Next the counselor or self-helping couple must define the problem, including the type of stress encountered and how one or both may have added to the difficulty. Open discussion is then encouraged, including free expression and nonjudgemental acceptance of thoughts and feelings, and topics may include the problem, methods of dealing with the problem, and aspects of the couple's dynamics.

Next, goals are identified and problem solving and communication techniques are implemented, including self-expression, listening, feedback, negotiation, acceptance, and dialogue. As these techniques are learned, many couples progress from Supportive or Nurturative to Unitive Levels of Interaction, as well as enhancing their stress adaptation mechanisms. Such changes raise the Couple Stability Index Value and the probability of couple continuation.

Whether they are working with a counselor or using self-help techniques, couples are aided by enlistment of family support, including biological, extended, or other effective family systems. Intervention may include bringing parents or children of the original couple partners into counseling, or enlisting their aid in times of crisis, as Roger and Gloria did.

PRESERVING THE COUPLES IN OUR LIVES

The couple is perhaps the central social unit in our society, the prototype of the family. The traditional family begins with the attraction and subsequent commitment of a man and woman, proceeds through marriage, childbearing, launching, and the post-parental years, so that in the end, after the children are gone, the family again consists of a man and woman—just two persons.

The rapid changes of the past two decades have included a dramatic rise in the rate of marriage termination so that now there is one divorce for each two marriages every year.[24] This decline in stability of the traditional marital union has been paralleled by a rise in alternative couple relationships, reflecting changing individual needs and shifts in cultural viewpoints concerning these unions. Today young men and women live together as couples openly, homosexual couples march militantly, and welfare mothers shun marrying their lovers to avoid loss of payments.

Both the individual and society have a stake in continuation of all types of couple associations. A basic human need filled by the couple relationship is companionship—the anodyne for loneliness. There is feedback concerning individual thoughts and actions. There is the knowledge that someone cares what happens. Antisocial activity is less commonly seen in individuals who enjoy a stable couple relationship, while psychopathic and antisocial acts are often ascribed to individuals who are lonely, socially isolated, and psychologically unsupported.

Analysis of couple stability allows identification of interpersonal problems and stresses which affect the relationship and permits intervention to anticipate and solve problems. Such assessment and intervention can help preserve couples in our lives, thus enhancing personal emotional well-being and social stability.

**COUPLE
FOCUS:
CHAPTER
TEN**

1. Can medical research models be used to measure human behavior?

2. How can the outcomes of couple continuation or termination be assessed?

3. What is the single aspect of the relationship that influences whether the couple stays together or splits?

4. How can couples improve the quality of their lives together?

CHAPTER TEN: OUTCOME AND THE QUALITY OF LIFE

10

IN THE WORLD OF SCIENCE, whenever a new theory is proposed, the proponents must wrestle with three questions: What is the outcome? How is it measured? Will it improve the quality of life?

Research in the traditional medical science model has emphasized the importance of numbers. What are the figures? How many patients are involved in the study? How many persons are in the control group? What is the dose and duration of treatment? What are the criteria by which results can be measured? What is the result of statistical analysis? For example, if one wishes to know the outcome of drug treatment of confused elderly persons, a research model might be: Treat 100 persons with the medication and compare them with a similar 100 persons who did not receive medication but who might be given similarly appearing inert tablets. Each of these groups might receive psychologic testing before and after drug use. Scientists and physicians feel right at home with such a research model. All results can be reduced to numbers which are then fed into the computer. In short order, results (outcomes) are presented in nice, neat, unassailable hard data.

But changes are occurring. Since the turn of the century the life expectancy in America has increased from a scant 49 years to exceed the proverbial three score years and ten. Tuberculosis, diphtheria, pneumonia and other infectious disease killers of the early 20th Century have been effectively conquered through vaccines and therapy, and today Americans are living to increasingly later ages. With increased longevity medical science is beginning to shift its research focus from *quantity* to *quality* of life. There is a growing body of opinion that holds that *how life is lived* is as important as the cure rates of bacterial pneumonia or the percentage of recovery following acute heart attack. A classic and dramatic example arises in the all-too-frequent example of the individual severely incapacitated following a stroke: Through heroic efforts, an aged individual may be snatched from death's door. The end result is an incapacitated, often bedfast, person with little response to his environment, kept alive by careful manipulation of fluids and tubes. In quantitative outcome analysis this patient is listed as a success. But when quality of life is considered, the outcome has been sad indeed.

We face analogous difficulties in assessing the outcome of couple continuity and, indeed, in validating the outcome of any behavioral or psychosocial interventions. Should the couple be preserved at all costs? Obviously not! When is couple termination a successful outcome? When is it a failure? If there was professional help, what interventions were used? In what doses? What would have happened in the absence of analysis and intervention, i.e. to a control couple? What was the outcome and how did it change the quality of life for the two persons involved?

The problem becomes simply: How does one keep score? How does one measure psychosocial outcomes and the quality of life? If the researcher wishes to go beyond the binary alternatives of survive vs. die, cure vs. fail, how does he keep score in a method that will be: (a) acceptable to colleagues and (b) reproducible by other researchers?

Behavioral scientists are only now beginning to address this problem and in the context of our couple continuity study let us present one model which—imperfect though it may be—can aid in analyzing the outcome of couple continuity.

Outcome: The Economic Model

Keeping score when a couple faces crisis could be done by many means: the number of fights per week, the number of nights spent crying, the number of therapy sessions, and so forth. As technology advances it may indeed be possible to measure minute changes in blood chemistries in relationship to stress. Indeed, some future scientist may evolve a scale by which to measure one's happiness level day by day.

Until that day comes we must keep score by other means. As society has progressed, the utilization of goods and services has changed from independence (when the cave-dweller was self-sufficient), to barter (when value was negotiated on an item by item basis), to the use of money (with generally accepted economic values determined by consensus). Therefore, by the law of supply and demand, influenced by cultural mores and governmental intervention, each good or service provided or consumed has some definable cost. Certainly the relentless march of inflation prevents assignment of absolute dollar values, yet relative values—let us say, the comparison between the cost of a loaf of bread and a bus ride—will remain similar.

Furthermore, as society has become more complex, social changes within the couple (or family) unit have come to involve changes in assets and utilization of goods and services which can be identified and subsequently quantified by identifying a dollar value. This then provides the basis for the economic model of outcome analysis.

The following stories of two very similar couples will illustrate the outcome impact of couple continuity vs. termination as expressed in terms of personal and societal benefits vs. costs, measured in dollars of relative value.

"Most likely to be married first" was the yearbook caption under the picture of Amy and Alan. And, in fact, the high school sweethearts fulfilled the prophecy, marrying soon after graduation. Alan took a job with a construction firm and Amy soon found that most of her time was spent caring for the two daughters that were born in the third and fourth years of marriage. Alan's salary and a bank mortgage allowed the purchase of a modest three bedroom house in a residential section of town.

The years passed, the children entered school, and Amy and Alan settled into the routine of family life. In the evening Alan would mow the lawn or trim the hedges while Amy fixed the family dinner. They might watch television or attend a family movie with the children, and on weekends they enjoyed relaxing at a lakeside beach where Alan would take their daughters boating while Amy lay in the sun.

Then came the inevitable choice and change. "An offer I can't refuse," is how Alan described the opportunity. His construction firm had been commissioned to build a major bridge in Brazil. The opportunity promised double pay for the duration of the project, estimated to be one year. Alan could almost feel the bonus money. But there was a catch. Workers on the project would be away from home until the job was finished.

Amy and Alan spent many hours discussing the advantages and disadvantages. Finally they decided: Alan would go. After planning and packing, amid tearful goodbys and promises to write daily, Alan left for Brazil.

As a result of storms, strikes, and illness the project seemed destined to continue forever, and during this time both Amy and Alan felt the effects of separation. The strain of being both mother and father to the girls began to tell on Amy, who became irritable and vaguely discontented with her life. Still attractive in her early 30s with flowing brown hair and a youthful figure, she began wondering just how she should respond to the friendly greetings of single males in the grocery store line.

Alan, too, found the separation and isolation from his family onerous. The glamour of the project soon faded and his loneliness eventually gave rise to despondency.

The couple continued to communicate by mail and by long-distance telephone calls as often as their budget would allow. Finally, after about nine months of separation, Amy wrote Alan a letter telling of her feelings of being attracted to other men, her sense of social isolation, and her concern for the future of their relationship. These concerns only intensified Alan's depression. It was agreed that Amy would speak with their family doctor, who in turn recommended counseling.

Amy's early sessions with the psychotherapist explored her values and goals and her early relationship with her parents. Then the therapist turned to her couple relationship with Alan—analyzing their interaction levels, their stage in the couple life cycle, and their family support systems. Finally came discussions of the separation stress she and Alan were experiencing and some helpful ways to cope.

Via long distance telephone calls they made their decision. The couple relationship was worth more than the bonus pay. Their quality of life was worth more than any quantity of dollars. Alan arranged with the company to end his work in Brazil and return to the United States, forsaking $7,000 in bonus pay.

He and Amy and their daughters cried at the airport reunion and spent the following week becoming reacquainted. Alan soon settled into his previous job at the home office, the bonus money he might have earned was soon forgotten, and once again he spent Sunday afternoons boating on the lake with his daughters.

Amy and Alan weathered a separation stress that could have split a less stable couple union. With the aid of professional counseling, the union and the source of stress were examined and methods were developed to meet the stress. Certainly, Alan's leaving his high paying job in Brazil represented a compromise, but one which all agreed was justified by the outcome.

Figure AA illustrates outcome analysis of Amy and Alan's couple story using the economic model. Note that there are significant personal and societal benefits to continuation of the couple union.

FIGURE AA: OUTCOME ANALYSIS
USING ECONOMIC MODEL

Amy and Alan: Continuation of Couple Relationship

Personal benefits vs (costs)	Dollar value
1. Cost of counseling	$ (200)
2. Loss of bonus pay	(7,000)
3. Preservation of intact family household/income (calculated as one half of family net worth)	15,000
Net personal value:	$ 7,800

Societal benefits vs (costs)	Dollar value
1. Increased taxes paid by intact couple/family unit (calculated as estimated increased federal, state, and local taxes paid by intact couple/family unit over 10 years)	$10,000
2. Value of volunteer/community service made possible by intact family unit	1,500
Net societal value:	$11,500

As shown in Figure AA couple continuation affords definite dollar benefits to the couple/family and to society. However, what also must be considered are the personal and societal drains of energy, time, and funds necessitated by the untimely ending of a couple relationship such as that of Beth and Bill.

Friends and neighbors often contrasted the problems of Beth and Bill with the solid family unit of Amy and Alan. In a sense, they almost served as what scientists call paired controls.

Beth and Bill had been in the same high school class as Amy and Alan, had also married soon after graduation, and were also parents of two children—a boy and a girl. Bill and Alan worked for the same construction company and Bill had also joined the Brazilian bridge project. Thus this couple faced the same prolonged separation stress as Amy and Alan.

However, the outcome was much different. Letters and telephone calls seemed to suffice until Bill had been away for seven months. The December holiday season approached and the children asked, "Why can't Daddy come home for Christmas? We haven't seen him in such a long time." Beth could only echo the children's sentiments. She had not seen her husband for what seemed eternity. Angry feeling began to rise. Is his job more important than me? Than us? Why does he feel he must earn the extra money? What is he doing in Brazil anyhow? Does he expect me just to sit home for a year and wait patiently?

When Christmas morning came and went without a card or gift from Bill, Beth decided, "I've had it. I can't take this anymore." She initiated, and Bill participated in, a long distance exchange of letters and telephone calls, blaming and punishing one another, with cutting rhetoric punctuated by pointed epithets.

Bill's judgment was firm: Leaving the job to return to his family would mean that he had been summoned home by his wife and that he had failed to complete his assignment. His sense of pride and duty kept him chained to the bridge until the first Brazilian car could roll across. He could not bend to meet Beth's needs.

At home Beth's needs for companionship, household help, and emotional support were not being met. She saw herself as trapped, and her situation did not promise to improve when an insensitive and stubborn husband returned five months hence. After much thought and following discussions with her mother and several close friends, Beth decided that divorce was the only answer.

She composed her letter to Bill very carefully, bravely assuming much of the blame, and hoping that they could part without rancor.

When Bill received the letter, it all seemed so far away and he could not be sure of Beth's intent. Was she serious or was the letter merely a ploy to bring him home, another salvo in the battle of blame and punishment? For whatever reasons, he took no action and stayed on the job in Brazil, while Beth proceeded with the divorce.

At the end of the following summer the bridge was finally completed, three months behind schedule. Bill said goodby to the Brazilian spiders and mosquitos, and returned home. The house that he and Beth had called home was being sold, and final papers for the divorce awaited his signature. Beth and the children had taken an apartment. He visited but there seemed to be a great distance between them. It had been such a long time since they had seen one another. So much had happened: During their separation their son had run away from home on two occasions and had become a behavior problem at school. Their daughter had developed a bedwetting problem and, after a thorough medical evaluation, had been referred for psychotherapy. Beth had a boyfriend who took the children to the park on weekends. It seemed to Bill that all that was left for him was to pay the lawyer's fee and find an apartment of his own.

The outcome of the Beth/Bill couple termination is analyzed in Figure BB.

FIGURE BB: OUTCOME ANALYSIS
USING ECONOMIC MODEL

Beth and Bill: Termination of Couple Relationship

Personal benefits vs (costs)	Dollar value
1. Legal fees: separation and divorce	$ (2,000)
2. Loss of intact family household/ income (calculated as one-half of family net worth	(15,000)
3. Psychotherapy: Beth	(400)
4. Private tutoring: both children	(600)
5. Added annual expense of maintaining two households	(5,000)
6. Beth: increased hours and wages received from new job	4,000
Net personal cost:	$(19,000)

Societal benefits vs. (costs)	Dollar value
1. Family Court services	$(5,000)
2. Police services	(1,000)
3. Mental Health Clinic counseling	(1,000)
4. Medical assistance	(1,000)
5. Loss of increased taxes paid by intact couple/family unit (calculated as estimated decreased federal, state, and local taxes paid by non-intact couple/family unit over 10 years)	(10,000)
Net societal cost:	$(18,000)

Outcome and the Quality of Life ● 171

As the couple relationship ended, Beth and Bill discovered that to the emotional upheaval of termination is added a significant dollar cost. Ending any couple relationship—marriage, partnership, corporation, and so forth—involving joint assets will result in an immediate loss to each couple member of the use of one half of these assets. Also to be considered is the high likelihood of the distress sale of a home or other valuable property. Calculations must consider the added expense of maintaining two separate households plus the cost treating emotional or behavioral problems arising as a consequence of the premature couple termination.

Society is also affected by the unexpected couple split. In the two examples cited, Amy and Alan continue to be contributing members of society while Beth and Bill become recipients of social services. During the many months of negotiation during separation and divorce Beth and Bill utilized Family Court services having an estimated value of $5,000. Their son's truancy and runaway episodes cost society $1,000, and another $2,000 in public funds (Beth and the children had qualified for Medicaid) was spent to deal with behavioral illnesses arising from the family crisis. Thus the couple termination resulted in Beth and Bill, on balance, taking more from society than they gave.

The economic outcome analysis underscores the fact that divorce is costly, a well known fact of life today. What is interesting is that the dollar costs of termination exceed the values ascribed to continuation. The difference lies in the cost of changes that must be made. Change is expensive—both economically and emotionally—and contemplation of the financial and psychological impact of couple termination may bring about a deeper assessment of the couple relationship.

The economic model of outcome analysis is but one example of how the behavioral sciences can be melded with the traditional research methods to assess outcome. The key is assigning numbers—values of some kind—to human behavior and events. But to do so is difficult and, indeed, highly problematic when considering the quality of human relationships.

The success or failure of couple stability analysis and intervention cannot be judged solely in dollars. Nor can it be judged by a head count of unions preserved. Somehow the outcome must be assessed according to the quality of life of the two persons involved—and of the relationship itself.

To this end we propose that the Couple Stability Index Value be used as a guide to the quality of couple life at any specific time. The interaction level, heavily weighted in the Couple Stability Index, is fundamental to the quality of life of two persons together. Also basic in analysis is knowledge of where the subject couple are in their couple life cycle, because this helps tell the extent to which stress will influence their life together. Since all of us are always under some stress, it helps to know the major couple stress and how this stress is being met, as well as the support being received from the effective family. Taken together and quantified, these five aspects of couple dynamics help tell the quality of couple life *at the time of analysis.*

Life changes, and so does the quality of life. When you began this book you completed a questionnaire concerning one of your couple relationships. To dramatize the changes that occur, you should perform two exercises:

1. Complete the same couple analysis (using the spaces provided in the appendix) for the same couple

relationship *one year ago*. What has changed? How do the couple stability index values differ? Is there correlation of the values and your subjective estimate of changes in the quality of couple life?

2.   Next complete another couple analysis after *both partners* have read this book. Has the book changed the couple interaction? Has it helped you identify your couple life stage or source of stress? Has it aided in dealing with a stress? Has it helped you to mobilize family or other support? Has your Couple Stability Index Value changed? Was reading this book an "intervention" and has your quality of couple life improved?

Elusive though its quantification may be, what keeps couples together is the quality of their relationship. And this in turn relates to the care and trust that is communicated to one another and to a willingness to face problems together. The key lies in communication; the effective interchange of thoughts and feelings enhances each facet of the couple relationship. Perhaps this book will provide a springboard to communication. We hope that we have sparked some interest in previously unexamined aspects of your couple relationships, and have started you talking about the quality of your life and of the unions that you share.

THE OUTCOME OF COUPLE DECISIONS CAN BE ASSESSED FOR COUPLES IN YOUR LIFE USING THE ECONOMIC MODEL. THIS MODEL ALLOWS ASSIGNMENT OF NUMERICAL (DOLLAR) VALUES TO EVENTS THAT OTHERWISE MIGHT BE HARD TO QUANTIFY. IT PRESUMES THAT ALTHOUGH THE COSTS OF GOODS AND SERVICES, SUCH AS COUNSELING FEES, WILL FLUCTUATE AND ALMOST INEVITABLY RISE, RELATIVE DOLLAR VALUES WILL REMAIN ROUGHLY PROPORTIONAL. THUS COUPLE STABILITY OUTCOME ANALYSIS CAN BE CALCULATED BY WRITING IN THE PERSONAL AND SOCIETAL BENEFITS OR COSTS OF ANY CONTEMPLATED ACTION AND ASSIGNING REALISTIC DOLLAR FIGURES.

COUPLE: _____

OUTCOME ANALYSIS: Continuation or separation

Personal benefits vs (costs)   Dollar value
    1. $
    2.
    3.
    4.
    5.
    6.   _____
            Net personal value (cost) $

Societal benefits vs (costs)   Dollar value
    1. $
    2.
    3.
    4.
    5.
    6.   _____
            Net societal value (cost) $

APPENDIX:

SYNOPSES OF COUPLE CASE STUDIES
and SELF-ANALYSIS TABLES

COUPLE STABILITY INDEX VALUES

Value Total	Couple Stability
+6 or greater	These couples have highly stable unions and will meet current stress with barely a ripple to disturb their relationships. They may indeed live "happily ever after."
+3 to +5	There is moderate stability to these unions, which will probably overcome problems without major crises.
+1 to +2	Couple bonds here are somewhat tenuous and major problems could endanger the union. Improved couple dynamics—including a deeper level of interaction and better ways of meeting stress—could enhance the relationship.
0	The future of these couples is uncertain. Their stability is borderline, and minor stress or shifts in adaptation could tip the scales for or against continuation.

-1 to -2	These couples lack stability and are likely to separate unless there is a change in couple dynamics.
-3 to -5	Significant problems exist in these relationships and separation is highly probable. Only hard work and skillful counseling offer hope of continuation.
-6 or less	These unions are almost certain to dissolve, and are probably past hope of saving. In fact, such relationships are often harmful to the individuals involved and probably should be terminated quickly and decisively.

TABLE 4: Harry and Jane

	Actual	Hypothetical: Dating
Interaction Level	+4	+2
Couple Life Stage	+1	+2
Stress Type	-3	-4
Stress Adaptation	+3	+2
Family Support	+2	0
	—	—
Couple Stability Index Value	+7	+2

COUPLE: HARRY AND JANE: Age mid-30's; married		Couple Stability Value
Couple Category I	Opposite sex Intragenerational Sexual	
Interaction Level	Unitive	+4
Couple Life Stage	Assessment	+1
Type of Stress	Values, roles and extra-couple relationships; Role change	-3
Stress Adaptation	Use of problemsolving and communication techniques	+3
Family Support	Families of both partners approve	+2
	Couple Stability Index Value	+7

TABLE 5: Roger and Gloria

Interaction Level	+3
Couple Life Stage	+4
Stress Type	-2
Stress Adaptation	-1
Family Support	+2
	—
Couple Stability Index Value	+6

COUPLE: ROGER AND GLORIA: Age mid-50's; restaurant owner and waitress		Couple Stability Value
Couple Category II	Opposite sex Intragenerational Asexual	
Interaction Level	Nurturative	+3
Couple Life Stage	Recommitment	+4
Type of Stress	Activity: change in working hours to include Sundays	-2
Stress Adaptation	Roger: Failure to confront problem (0) Gloria: Rigidification (-1)	-1
Family Support	Effective family support of relationship	+2
	Couple Stability Index Value	+6

TABLE 6: John and Margaret

	Actual	Hypothetical: Major Stress in Assessment Stage
Interaction Level	+2	+2
Couple Life Stage	+3	+1
Stress Type	-1	-4
Stress Adaptation	+2	+2
Family Support	-1	-1
	—	—
Couple Stability Index Value	+5	0

COUPLE:	JOHN AND MARGARET: John, age 53, and Margaret, age 25, second marriage for both	Couple Stability Value
Couple Category III	Opposite sex Intergenerational Sexual	
Interaction Level	Supportive	+2
Couple Life Stage	Commitment	+3
Type of Stress	Object: Buying a house	-1
Stress Adaptation	Open discussion by both	+2
Family Support	John: Family disapproval (-1) Margaret: Effective family ambivalent (0)	-1
	Couple Stability Index Value	+5

TABLE 7: Joseph and Maria

Interaction Level	+1
Couple Life Stage	+2
Stress Type	-4
Stress Adaptation	+2
Family Support	-2
Couple Stability Index Value	-1

COUPLE:	JOSEPH AND MARIA: Joseph, age 72, is father of Maria, age 36	Couple Stability Value
Couple Category IV	Opposite sex Intergenerational Asexual	
Interaction Level	Convenient	+1
Couple Life Stage	Accommodation	+2
Type of Stress	Couple Unity: Maria receives a proposal of marriage	-4
Stress Adaptation	Both recognize problem and discuss possible outcome	+2
Family Support	Peer and extended family disapproval of father/daughter couple relationship	-2
	Couple Stability Index Value	-1

TABLE 8: George and Frank

Interaction Level	+3
Couple Life Stage	+4
Stress Type	-1
Stress Adaptation	0
Family Support	-2
	—
Couple Stability Index Value	+4

COUPLE: GEORGE AND FRANK: Both in late 40's		Couple Stability Value
Couple Category V	Same sex Intragenerational Sexual	
Interaction Level	Nurturative	+3
Couple Life Stage	Recommitment	+4
Type of Stress	Object: Frank using couple's money to help pay son's college tuition	-1
Stress Adaptation	Frank: Recognizes problem (+1) George: Transference (-1)	0
Family Support	Both families disapprove of couple relationship	-2
	Couple Stability Index Value	-4

TABLE 9: Charles and Michael

	Actual	Hypothetical: Problem Solving
Interaction Level	+1	+1
Couple Life Stage	+2	+2
Stress Type	-2	-2
Stress Adaptation	-2	+3
Family Support	0	0
	—	—
Couple Stability Index Value	-1	+4

COUPLE:	CHARLES AND MICHAEL: Both in late teens, college roommates	Couple Stability Value
Couple Category VI	Same sex Intragenerational Asexual	
Interaction Level	Convenience	+1
Couple Life Stage	Accommodation	+2
Type of Stress	Activity: Charles prefers loud music, late hours; Michael can study only in quiet atmosphere	-2
Stress Adaptation	Both: Frequent arguments without resolution	-2
Family Support	Charles' family believes Michael will be good influence (+1); Michael's family disapprove of Charles' lifestyle (-1)	0
	Couple Stability Index Value	-1

TABLE 10: Phyllis and Nancy

	Actual	Hypothetical: Early Stress Met Poorly
Interaction Level	+4	+2
Couple Life Stage	+1	+1
Stress Type	-4	-4
Stress Adaptation	+3	-2
Family Support	0	0
Couple Stability Index Value	+4	-3

COUPLE: PHYLLIS AND NANCY:
Phyllis, age 48, college profes-   Couple Stability
sor; Nancy, age 22, her stu-   Value
dent

		Couple Stability Value
Couple Category VII	Same sex Intragenerational Sexual	
Interaction Level	Unitive	+4
Couple Life Stage	Assessment	+1
Type of Stress	Couple Unity: Separation following Nancy's graduation	-4
Stress Adaptation	Communication techniques: Letters and journals	+3
Family Support	Phyllis: Family/peer approval (+1) Nancy: Family disapprove (-1)	0
	Couple Stability Index Value	+4

TABLE 11: Lucille and Martha

Interaction Level	+2
Couple Life Stage	+3
Stress Type	-3
Stress Adaptation	0
Family Support	+1
	——
Couple Stability Index Value	+3

COUPLE: LUCILLE AND MARTHA:

	Lucille, age 62, and her divorced daughter Martha, age 39	Couple Stability Value
Couple Category VIII	Same sex Intergenerational Asexual	
Interaction Level	Supportive	+2
Couple Life Stage	Commitment	+3
Type of Stress	Values, roles, and extra-couple relationships: Childrearing	-3
Stress Adaptation	Both fail to face problem	0
Family Support	Lucille: Family/peer indifference (0); Martha: Children approve (+1)	+1
	Couple Stability Index Value	+3

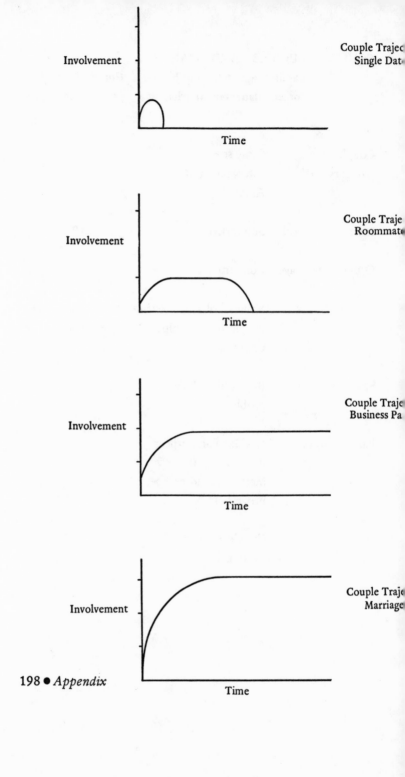

Couple Traject
Single Date

Couple Traje
Roommate

Couple Traje
Business Pa

Couple Traje
Marriage

198 ● *Appendix*

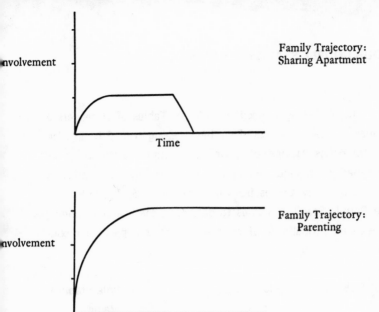

Involvement

Time

Family Trajectory:
Sharing Apartment

Involvement

Time

Family Trajectory:
Parenting

YOUR COUPLE STABILITY INDEX

The following blank Self-Analysis Tables offer readers a chance to analyze couples they belong to. Fill in the characteristics of one of your own couple relationships as described throughout this book. Then fill in the applicable Couple Stability Values from chapters 4, 5, 6, 7, and 8. Add the Couple Stability Values to determine the Couple Stability Index—the probability of continuing for that particular couple.

COUPLE: _____ and _____   Couple Stability
                                                  Value

Couple Category _____

Interaction Level

Couple Life Stage

Type of Stress

Stress Adaptation

Family Support

Couple Stability Index Value

YOUR COUPLE STABILITY INDEX

The following blank Self-Analysis Tables offer readers a chance to analyze couples they belong to. Fill in the characteristics of one of your own couple relationships as described throughout this book. Then fill in the applicable Couple Stability Values from chapters 4, 5, 6, 7, and 8. Add the Couple Stability Values to determine the Couple Stability Index—the probability of continuing for that particular couple.

COUPLE: _____ and _____   Couple Stability
                                                                          Value

---

Couple Category _____

Interaction Level

Couple Life Stage

Type of Stress

Stress Adaptation

Family Support

Couple Stability Index Value

YOUR COUPLE STABILITY INDEX

The following blank Self-Analysis Tables offer readers a chance to analyze couples they belong to. Fill in the characteristics of one of your own couple relationships as described throughout this book. Then fill in the applicable Couple Stability Values from chapters 4, 5, 6, 7, and 8. Add the Couple Stability Values to determine the Couple Stability Index—the probability of continuing for that particular couple.

COUPLE: _____ and _____

	Couple Stability Value
Couple Category _____	
Interaction Level	
Couple Life Stage	
Type of Stress	
Stress Adaptation	
Family Support	
Couple Stability Index Value	

YOUR COUPLE STABILITY INDEX

The following blank Self-Analysis Tables offer readers a chance to analyze couples they belong to. Fill in the characteristics of one of your own couple relationships as described throughout this book. Then fill in the applicable Couple Stability Values from chapters 4, 5, 6, 7, and 8. Add the Couple Stability Values to determine the Couple Stability Index—the probability of continuing for that particular couple.

COUPLE: _____ and _____

Couple Stability
Value

Couple Category _____

Interaction Level

Couple Life Stage

Type of Stress

Stress Adaptation

Family Support

Couple Stability Index Value

YOUR COUPLE STABILITY INDEX

The following blank Self-Analysis Tables offer readers a chance to analyze couples they belong to. Fill in the characteristics of one of your own couple relationships as described throughout this book. Then fill in the applicable Couple Stability Values from chapters 4, 5, 6, 7, and 8. Add the Couple Stability Values to determine the Couple Stability Index—the probability of continuing for that particular couple.

COUPLE: _____ and _____   Couple Stability
                                                                                           Value

_____

Couple Category _____

Interaction Level

Couple Life Stage

Type of Stress

Stress Adaptation

Family Support

_____

Couple Stability Index Value

YOUR COUPLE STABILITY INDEX

The following blank Self-Analysis Tables offer readers a chance to analyze couples they belong to. Fill in the characteristics of one of your own couple relationships as described throughout this book. Then fill in the applicable Couple Stability Values from chapters 4, 5, 6, 7, and 8. Add the Couple Stability Values to determine the Couple Stability Index—the probability of continuing for that particular couple.

COUPLE: _____ and _____   Couple Stability
                                           Value

Couple Category _____

Interaction Level

Couple Life Stage

Type of Stress

Stress Adaptation

Family Support

Couple Stability Index Value

REFERENCES

1. Binger, C. M., A. R. Albin, R. C. Feurstein, J. H. Kushner, and C. Mikkelsen. Childhood Leukemia Emotional Impact on Patient and Family. N.Eng.Jour.Med., 280:414-418, 1969.
2. Carmichael, I. P. The Family in Medicine, Process or Entity. J.Fam.Prac., 3:562-563, 1976.
3. Crain, A. J. Effects of a Diabetic Child on Marital Integration and Related Measures of Family Function. Journal of Health and Human Behavior, 7:122-127, 1966.
4. Gallagher, Father Chuck. The Marriage Encounter. New York, Doubleday, 1975.
5. Hill, R. Generic Features of Families under Stress. Social Casework, 39:139-150, 1958.
6. Holmes T. H. and R. D. Rahe. The Social Readjustment Rating Scale. Journal of Psychomatic Research, 11:213-218, 1967.
7. Howells, J. G. Principles of Family Psychiatry. New York, Brunner/Mazel, 1975.
8. Kluckholn, F. R. Variations in the Basic Values of Family Systems. Social Casework, 11:213-216, 1958.
9. Koch J. and L. Koch. The Marriage Savers. New York, Coward, McCann and Goeghegan, 1976.

10. Laswell M. and N. Lobsenz. No Fault Marriage. New York, Doubleday, 1976.

11. Leaverton, D. R. "The Child with Diabetes Mellitus." In Noshptiz, J. (ed.). Basic Handbook of Child Psychiatry. New York, Basic Books, 1977.

12. Mace, D. R. Success in Marriage. Nashville, Abingdon Press, 1958.

13. Martin, P. A. A Marital Therapy Manual. New York, Brunner/Mazel, 1976.

14. McGinnis, T. C. and J. V. Ayres. Open Family Living. New York, Doubleday, 1976.

15. Minuchin, A. Families and Family Therapy. Boston, Harvard University Press, 1974.

16. Ransom, D. C. and H. E. Vandervoort. The Development of Family Medicine. JAMA, 225:1098-1102, 1973.

17. Rothus, S. A. and J. S. Nevid. BT (Behavior Therapy). New York, Doubleday, 1977.

18. Sheehy, G. Passages. New York, E.P. Dutton, 1976.

19. Taylor, R. B. Doctor Taylor's Self-Help Medical Guide. New Rochelle, N.Y., Arlington House, 1977.

20. Taylor, R. B. Feeling Alive After 65. New Rochelle, N.Y., Arlington House, 1973.

21. Taylor, R. B. Welcome to the Middle Years. Washington, D.C., Acropolis Books, 1977.

22. Turk, J. Impact of Cystic Fibrosis on Family Functioning. Pediatrics, 34:67-71, 1964.

23. Vital Statistics Report: Final Divorce Statistics 1975. National Center for Health Statistics, Rockville, Md., Vol. 26, No. 2, Supplement 2, May 19, 1977.

24. Vital Statistics Report. HRA 77-1120, Vol. 26, No. 8, National Center for Health Statistics, Rockville, Md., Nov. 9, 1977.